OTHELLO

a novel

OTHELLO

a novel

by

JULIUS
LESTER

SCHOLASTIC
HARDCOVER

Scholastic Inc. New York

For information regarding permission, write to Scholastic Inc.,
555 Broadway, New York, NY 10012.

Library of Congress Cataloging-in-Publication Data

Lester, Julius
Othello: a novel / by Julius Lester
p. cm.
Summary: A prose retelling of Shakespeare's play in which a
jealous general is duped into thinking that his wife
has been unfaithful, with tragic consequences.
ISBN 0-590-41967-6
1. Shakespeare, William, 1564–1616 —
Characters — Othello — Juvenile Fiction.
[1. Shakespeare, William, 1564–1616 — Adaptations.]
I. Shakespeare, William, 1564–1616.
Othello. II. Title.
PR2878.O8L47   1995
813'.54 — dc20   94-12833
                                                            CIP
                                                            AC

12 11 10 9 8 7 6 5 4 3 2 1   5 6 7 8 9/9 0/0

Printed in the U.S.A.   37

First Scholastic printing, April 1995

Designed by Elizabeth B. Parisi

To Milan,
another one for you

Contents

Introduction

In the characters of William Shakespeare's plays we find vivid representations of the inner human landscape that is part of all of us. Romeo and Juliet, Hamlet and Ophelia, Macbeth and Lady Macbeth, Othello and Iago, Julius Caesar and Brutus, and other characters transcend the plays to which they belong. Romeo and Juliet, for example, are the purest examples of romantic lovers in the English language, and at some time, most of us have imagined ourselves to be one or the other. Iago is jealousy incarnate, while Lady Macbeth's ruthlessness attracts and repels us simultaneously, as perhaps does our own capacity for ruthlessness.

It is therefore more than unfortunate that Shakespeare's plays are increasingly inaccessible to many because of its unfamiliar and difficult language. Elizabethan English is almost a foreign tongue compared to the English of today, making it a challenge to read Shakespeare without explanatory footnotes.

Most are forced to read Shakespeare in high school or college, but once the final exam is over, many never read or see a play of his again (except for the film versions of *Hamlet* or *Romeo and Juliet*, which seem to be made at least once each decade). But Shakespeare was a playwright as eager to get people into the theater as a movie producer today wants a box-office hit. How ironic that Shakespeare has become the almost exclusive property of scholars.

Yet, the human dramas enacted in his plays continue to be enacted in our lives. We still see ourselves as Romeo and Juliet seeking the perfect love. In our trying times we find ourselves asking, like Hamlet, "To be or not to be: that is the question." *Othello: A Novel* is an attempt to blend Shakespeare's characters and story with more accessible English and a reworking of the characters.

What does that mean? How is this novel similar to and different from Shakespeare's *Othello*?

First, this is a novel; the original is a play. A novel is private and intimate, one individual — the writer — speaking to another individual — the reader. A play is a public event. It is designed not to be read but to be seen. A play is a collaboration between playwright, actors, director, producer, and the skilled craftspeople needed to mount a play successfully. In a play, time is generally the present, even if the play is set in the past. In a novel time is more like a spiral, moving back and forth along a continuum. A play (at least on the page) depends entirely on soliloquy and dialogue. A novel uses descriptions and interior monologues, as well as dialogue.

Because this is a novel, there were demands

to be met that would not be a problem in a play. Chief of these was historicity. In the theater we are willing to suspend disbelief and use our imaginations to transform a spare stage setting into a castle or ship or tenement house. In a novel, however, we expect to be rooted in time and place by descriptions.

Shakespeare's *Othello* is set in Venice and Cyprus. Because there is nothing in the play that says it must be set in Venice and Cyprus, I set the novel in late fifteenth- to early sixteenth-century England because it made everything historically simpler for me as a writer. (Other plays — *Romeo and Juliet* and *The Merchant of Venice* — could not be moved from Italy so easily.)

The major difference between this novel and the play is in my characterization of the central characters, Othello and Iago. Shakespeare's Othello is described as a "moor," the Elizabethan generic word for someone black or swarthy. Shakespeare invests Othello with great dignity and there is certainly nothing racist in how the character is written. Yet the references to Othello's blackness made by Iago, Othello himself, and other characters are all negative.

Presumably Shakespeare depicts Othello as black because he was a "moor" in the novel from which Shakespeare took the story. But Othello's race is not crucial to the unfolding of the tragedy. There were no Africans in Elizabethan England. Occasionally, one would be brought through London and put on display as an oddity, but one can perhaps safely say that Shakespeare had no contact with Africans. Making his character African was a way to get people into the theater. But Shakespeare's Othello is deracinated, i.e., besides his skin color there is nothing African about him.

When I began, I had thought I would write a novelization of Shakespeare's *Othello*, a book that could act as an introduction and bridge to the play itself for readers unable to make the connection directly. However, as I began writing, I found myself asking some very practical questions, questions I wanted answers to if the novel was to have its own integrity. Here, too, is another difference between fiction and theater. In the theater, we not only suspend disbelief, we give ourselves permission to become totally involved in the play. Contradictions, things that don't quite fit, either pass us by or we forgive because we want to stay in the moment of the play. With a novel, however, we stop and say, "Wait a minute. That doesn't make sense." With a novel we turn back a few pages to see if we missed something, or if something said on page 52 contradicts what we just read on page 68.

Some of the questions I wanted answers to were:

How did Othello get to England? How had he adjusted to life there? Did he miss his homeland? What had his homeland been like? Who had he been in his homeland? What was his name in Africa? Did he think of himself as European or African, or both? These were not questions for Shakespeare and his time, but they are very logical ones for ours.

The most radical departure from the play was my decision to make Iago and his wife, Emilia, African. If race was going to be more central in the novel, and it was, Iago could not be white, because his jealousy might stereotype him as a racist. I found it more interesting to explore racist feelings in a black person.

Another question was whether to use any of Shakespeare's language. But how could one *not* use language so extraordinary? I have made use of Shakespeare's language in several ways: (1) exactly as it appears in the play; (2) by paraphrasing if there are allusions in the original that reflect Elizabethan society in a way not readily comprehensible now; (3) by putting images, concepts, and syntax in a more contemporary context. Phrases, sentences, and passages based on Shakespeare will be recognizable because they are in another typeface.

Examples:

Shakespeare: ... to the sooty bosom of such a thing as thou.

Revision: **... to the sooty bosom of such a thing as you.**

Shakespeare: He is a soldier fit to stand by Caesar And give direction; and do but see his vice; 'Tis to his virtue a just equinox....

Revision: Despite his lack of experience he is a soldier fit to stand by Caesar. Yet his vice is the same length as his virtue like shadow and sunlight at the moment of the equinox.

Shakespeare: But I do think it is their husbands' faults
If wives do fall: say that they slack their duties
And pour our treasures into foreign laps,
Or else break out in peevish jealousies,
Throwing restraint upon us, or say they strike us,
Or scant our former having in despite,
Why, we have galls, and though we have some grace,
Yet have we some revenge....

Revision: If you really want to know what I think, well, I think it is their husbands' faults if wives are untrue. It is they who curdle the milk with their suspicions and jealousies. It is they who want to keep us locked away from an admiring eye or a covetous and innocent smile. It is they who strike us when we will not take the bridles with which they seek to rein us. They do not think we are capable of anger and resentment. They do not think we would seek revenge on them as they would seek revenge on one who injured them in spirit or body....

It is my hope that those who might feel intimidated by Shakespeare will gain sufficient confidence from this exposure to his language to read the original for themselves. It is also my hope that those who are comfortable with Shakespeare will find a new pleasure in this reimagining.

This novel is not intended to be a substitute for Shakespeare's *Othello*. It is a work in and of itself. While I follow the basic plot and dramatic line of the play, many of the characters' motivations are different. There are also characters and story lines in the novel that do not appear in the play; most prominent are the King and Desdemona's mother. I also have omitted from the novel characters in the play, namely the senators whose dramatic functions were given to the King's entourage. Additionally, there are scenes and changes of scenes in the novel not found in the play. This is not, therefore, a translation of Shakespeare's *Othello* into modern English. This is a reconceptualization, bringing Othello's race and questions of identity and psychic dislocation together with Shakespeare's own questions about appearance and reality.

In reality I am doing as Shakespeare himself did. Shakespeare took his stories and plots from other works. *Othello* is believed to be from an Italian novel, *Il Moro de Venezia*, by Giraldi Cinthio. Shakespeare changed the novel to explore a corner of the human soul as well as to fit the requirements of the stage and an audience. I have taken the play and created a novel in an attempt to do the same.

JULIUS LESTER
February 9, 1994
Belchertown, Massachusetts

OTHELLO

a novel

Chapter One

Desdemona

All morning she had sat in the window seat of her room. Looking down into the courtyard of the castle she could see peasants hurrying back and forth from the storehouse to the kitchen. The soldiers were returning, and once again the Great Hall would be loud with laughter and singing. And once again, she would take her place between her father and *him* at the table.

Desdemona turned her gaze outward beyond the castle walls. The castle sat on the crest of a hill. A broad road with trees bordering either side led from the gates to the lip of the crest. From there the road twisted and turned around the mountain to the village at the bottom. Her grandfather had built the castle in times more fierce than this. Fear of enemies, not convenience, had dictated his choice of where to build. Now, when enemies were few, all that remained, according to Desdemona's father, was the inconvenience. She supposed he was right. The ride up the mountain was difficult, especially when it rained. But once you reached the top, the sight of the broad, straight avenue and the towering castle at its end rested the spirit as few vistas she had ever seen.

Sometime that afternoon the men would ride over the crest and onto the avenue. From how they rode she would be able to tell if there had been a battle and how they had fared. Not that she could recall a time they had not returned in triumph during the year since the King had had them housed there.

Only a year? she mused. How could that be? She had known Othello for only a year? But memories of him permeated all her sixteen years. She knew intellectually that she had not known him even when her mother died almost two years ago; yet, when she thought of that time, she could see him standing by the bier. Love had remade her past as if it were a drab suitor in need of a velvet cape.

But did she dare call what she felt love? And was it truly love if it was not returned? She *thought* he liked her. He had indicated as much in the message Michael Cassio had brought her on his behalf before they left a month ago. But in the life of a young woman, a month was more than enough time for doubt to become as plentiful as pollen. What could he see in her who had never been farther than London? He had lived twice as long and seen more of the world than she knew there was to dream of. Oh, how she loved to hear his stories of the strange places and strange customs he had seen. Being with him was a continual adventure.

Just then she saw a figure on a horse come over the crest of the hill. Immediately after came other riders.

"They're here!" she shouted. They were too far away to identify anyone, but she knew Othello would be somewhere in the middle, if not at the rear.

Others of his rank would have ridden triumphantly at the head of their troops as if they were the proud bobbing head of a well-groomed but spoiled horse. Not Othello. He disdained the mane of commander. He needed no other title than *Othello*. To her his name was like a wreath woven from the scents of flowers and hum of bees.

"Emily!" she shouted. "They're back!"

A woman the color of burnt cinnamon rose from the stool before the fireplace. Carefully, she folded the garment she had been sewing and laid it at the foot of the bed. She was a small woman, or she appeared so with her black hair cut close to her head. Yet, when she went to the window and stood beside Desdemona, who, in her excitement, had forsaken her perch, the two were of almost equal height. Yet Desdemona, with black hair falling like silken rain to her waist, appeared the taller. But there was no mistaking who was the older. Though Emily had lived a mere ten years more than the one whose cheeks flamed crimson with love, her quiet self-containment gave her the appearance of an elegant maturity the younger woman would not attain even in a century of decades.

"Iago rides in front," Desdemona said to Emily.

Emily looked. Why was he riding there, she wondered, and not in his place beside Othello? Had something happened? If so, he would probably never tell her what and why.

Desdemona looked at Iago without expression. He and Othello were darker than Emily, as dark as night. Yet his blackness made her fearful where Othello's did not. She did not understand and did not think it important enough to reflect on. He was only Emily's husband to her, but Emily was the woman who had filled some of the emptiness left by the death of her mother. Iago was also the aide-de-camp to Othello, their friendship going back to Africa. Both were giants of men, as if their bodies disdained earth and longed to, at the least, brush the bottom of the sky. But where Othello's voice burst from him with the eagerness of the sun from its night chamber, Iago's seemed to slide forth like a serpent from its hole after winter's passage. If she had thought about it, she would have known that he frightened her. But because he was loved by Emily and Othello, there was no reason to reflect on her emotions about him.

Her eyes next found Michael and a smile returned. They had known each other since they were small children. Everyone had assumed she and Michael would marry one day. Oddly, neither she nor Michael had ever assumed that. Love requires the unsolvable mystery of two unknowns calling for completion in the other. She and Michael were more like two puppies playing together in the grass.

Since her mother's death Lord Bertrand, her father, had been eager for her to marry. How many times she had sat in the window seat and watched a young man ride down the avenue intent on gaining entrance to her heart with lute songs, poems, or perfumes from distant and exotic lands. To her father's disappointment, and now chagrin, she had turned each away. Although they were handsome, of good families, wealthy, and would be powerful men one day, none of that was important to her.

"The man I marry must *matter* to me, Father," she had tried to explain. "I want to greet each day with love burning as fiercely as the pain in the arrow-pierced heart of a deer." Lord Bertrand had groaned audibly. So she did not tell him she had met a man to whom she would gladly give her heart for him to hold in the palm of his hand and crush in the vise of his fist.

There he was now, his thighs clasping the horse's flank. Death could have taken her soul if, at that moment, God had made her into the horse.

"I suppose I should go down and see if there is anything my husband requires," Emily said softly.

Othello looked up as if he had known Desdemona's eyes were on him. Startled, she could not look away. She stared back at him until he vanished through the castle gate.

Chapter Two

Michael Pays a Visit

"I wore the green one at the banquet my father held before the men left. I look and feel like a child in it. It makes me appear flat where I am now quite round."

Emily gazed at the girl with bemused bewilderment. It could not have been longer ago than that morning, or certainly not later than the day before, that she had sat on the child's bed, looked into those blue eyes, and told her stories of the kings of Africa.

What happened? Had Emily blinked her eyes and in the darkness of the blinking the gods had substituted this beautiful young woman for the child that had been there the moment before? Emily knew better; yet, the change from child to woman and the change from man to old man seemed to take place with the suddenness of an unanticipated death.

When she had gone down to the courtyard to welcome her husband she had been startled to see an old African at the well outside the soldiers' barracks. She wondered who he was and why he had returned with them. Then, as she came closer, she was embarrassed and ashamed to recognize Iago. She was too young to blame aging eyes. Neither could she pretend that the sun had blinded her. Something had happened. Age had surprised and gathered him like an old woman gathers flowers and weeds for her poultices.

"I will wear the black one. It is cut low enough and tightly enough to attract his eye, yet high enough to conceal. Also, the black color will emphasize the paleness of my skin. Do you think he will find me immodest? Say something. You have known him practically all your life."

"Lord Bertrand might not approve of your appearing in the hall in such a gown."

"My father will not notice."

"Do not be sure. A father who has only one child, and that one a daughter, knows every hair of her head and precisely where it lies. Or is supposed to."

There was a knock at the door.

"Who could that be?" Emily asked.

"I know whom I wish it were but, in all likelihood, it is Michael."

"Yes, of course," Emily said, going to open the door.

"Emily," said the young man standing there.

"It is good to see you," she responded with a slight curtsy.

"Is Des — "

"And where else would I be? Come in, come in. Perhaps you can help me decide what I should wear tonight."

Michael entered the room with all the eagerness of young love. But if any stranger observing had thought it was love for the young woman who greeted him with a warm hug and quick kisses on each cheek, that stranger would have been mistaken. His eagerness was nothing more than an expression of his youthful delight in life, and on this particular afternoon, his eagerness was as unrestrained as a spring breeze.

"I have wonderful news, Desdemona."

"What holds your tongue?"

"Othello has promoted me to lieutenant!"

"Oh, Michael!" Desdemona exclaimed, giving him another hug.

"Congratulations," Emily said with strained warmth. "You must have acquitted yourself well in the recent battles for the General to have promoted you past men your senior." *Is that why Iago looked old and vanquished?* she asked herself.

"There was no battle," the young man responded.

"No battle?" the two women said almost simultaneously.

"None, I tell you. When the Duke of Leceister saw that the King had sent Othello to do battle, the Duke thought it best to make arrangements to pay his taxes to the King. We spent the time as guests of the Duke while he and the King's councillors made their peace. Even now the King himself is visiting with the Duke and will be here the day after tomorrow to visit with Lord Bertrand."

"The King! Here? This is some kind of joke."

"I swear!" Michael exclaimed. "The King will be here the day after tomorrow."

"Pardon me," Emily interrupted quietly. "You were going to tell us how you became Othello's lieutenant."

"Yes. Of course. There is not very much to tell. I knew nothing of it before Othello rose from his seat at the banquet table the night before we left the Duke's. He raised his goblet. We did the same, and he said he wanted to offer a toast to his new lieutenant, Michael Cassio. No one was more shocked and surprised than I. If he had spoken to me in private I would have reminded him that I did not have battlefield experience. Quite frankly I feel I am too young to be in charge of men older and battle tested."

"Nonsense!" Desdemona said emphatically. "Othello recognizes that you are a born leader. Virtue counts for more than valor, Michael, and you wear virtue like angels' wings."

"Thank you. I will certainly do nothing to violate Othello's faith in me. I will be the best lieutenant he has ever had."

"How did the men receive the news?" Emily wanted to know.

"Surprisingly well. And no one was more enthusiastic and supportive than your Iago."

"Is that so?"

"Indeed. He was the first to offer a toast after

Othello sat down. Afterwards he took me aside and said Othello could not have made a better selection. Iago has been most helpful with his counsel."

"I am glad to hear it," Emily said, though there was no gladness in her voice.

The two young people eased themselves toward the far corner of the room to whisper where they would not be overheard. Emily sat down on the stool before the cold fireplace. She ached for her husband's pain. And she feared it. Pain that could not be assuaged became fury that seared the soul like the bitter cold of the northern climes burned the skin with frozen heat.

For the fourteen years the three of them had been together she had watched Iago trying to grow toward the sunlight within the long shadows cast by Othello. While everyone recognized and extolled Othello's battlefield exploits, military planning, and strategies, Iago's contributions went unacknowledged, even by Othello. When Othello rewarded men after a battle, Iago was never one of them. Emily thought she understood why. Othello's sense of honor and propriety would not allow him to draw attention to Iago lest it appear he were favoring one with whom he shared color of skin. It was a noble gesture, but was nobility upheld at the expense of another's self-esteem?

"Emily! Emily!" Desdemona shouted from across the room. "Did you hear?"

"No. What?"

The two young people hurried toward the older woman, both blushing and giggling. "Go on, Michael. Tell her. Tell her."

"Well, last evening after we made camp, Othello came to me. He is not a man of many words. I perceive a shyness in him, which I find odd in one who has risked his life in the bloodiest of battles."

"Action is a language of immediacy," Emily explained. "Words, however, seldom say what they mean. They can make truth appear false and lies proclaim a truth that never was. A sword is a language whose truth cannot be disguised, hidden, or falsified."

"You speak like a warrior, Emily."

"A warrior's wife must understand the ways of war. But forgive me. I interrupted you."

"Well, it took him a while to get to the point but finally he asked me, 'Is the lady Desdemona promised to anyone? It seems that many expect the two of you to marry.' I told him that Desdemona and I knew each other far too well to risk marriage. As for others, practically every man in the kingdom had presented himself to her but she remained unpromised. He was silent for a long while. When he finally spoke it was in a voice of such soft tenderness that it almost brought tears to my eyes:

" 'I am not as young as I was once. The days when I can lead men into battle are numbered. When I look back at my life I see that my legacy is corpses. When I look forward I see an emptiness as silent as the emptiness to which I consigned so many. Until now, however, I never had time to think of marriage or family. In all truth, my friend, I do not know if I would be thinking of these things now if not for Desdemona. I find myself looking forward to the times when I am at my manor house on her father's estate and come to the castle to dine because I will see her. I look forward to her laughter bright as starshine. When I am in her presence, I wish I could banish the gray from this beard and the dust from this soul.' He was silent again. Finally, he looked at me. 'Michael Cassio. You know her well. If you think it wise and prudent, tell her that if she is not repulsed by one almost old enough to be her father and as black as the unknown, that one would be honored by the opportunity for her to know him better.' He turned and walked away. It was as if he did not want to hear my answer, afraid I would refuse him. I would never have refused his request. I know of no man I would more like to see Desdemona married to."

"And there is no man I would rather marry," Desdemona responded with such unguarded emotion that Emily feared her own heart would break.

Chapter Three

Othello and Desdemona in the Great Hall

The Great Hall was enormous enough to seat more than a hundred at meals, and yet leave space for strolling musicians, jugglers, and jesters to walk among the guests. At the front a raised platform covered twenty of the hall's thirty-five-foot width. On it rested three long tables covered with white tablecloths. These were reserved for Lord Bertrand, his steward and clerks, and visiting dignitaries. At the center were two carved high-backed chairs reserved for Lord Bertrand and, when she was alive, Lady Beatrice. That chair was now Desdemona's. Everyone else sat on benches.

Othello looked out over the hall at tables on each side that extended almost the hundred-foot length of the room. These tables were not dignified by tablecloths and their rough wooden surfaces were stained by years of spilled sauces, gravies, and the fat and juices of meats and fowls and venison. Benches sat on both sides of the tables and tonight, with the return of the soldiers, there was scarcely an empty spot to be found. Othello was amazed at how many people were required to see to the needs of the castle:

the marshall with his staff of grooms, pages, and maids to keep the castle in a reasonable state of cleanliness; the butler and pantler who were responsible for keeping the castle supplied with food and drink. There was even someone called a ewer, whose job was to clean the white tablecloths. There were also serving maids, cooks, carpenters, blacksmiths, grooms to care for the horses, gardeners to tend the vegetables and flowers, sweepers who kept the courtyards clean, peasants who saw to the chickens and livestock. Others went through the castle each week taking down the tapestries that covered the walls of almost every room and shook them free of dust, lice, and fleas. Othello reserved his deepest sympathies, however, for those who had to shovel out the latrines.

He sipped from a bowl of wine and wondered if Modibo and Ashaki were not right: Perhaps it *was* time they returned to Africa. As closely as he could figure he had been in Europe twenty years — nearly half his life, he figured. Yet, in all that time, he had never forgotten who he was and from whence he had come. When the three of them were alone, they made a point of addressing each other by the names given them by their parents: Iago was once again Modibo — Helper. Emily became Ashaki — Beautiful. And, to them he was Enaharo — Like the Sun. However, was he still Enaharo to himself?

He was not sure. There was much about Europeans that he despised. The floors of their castles and houses were covered with rushes and grasses and herbs. On the day these were spread, they filled the air with a pleasant aroma. But they were also filled with fleas and gnats and other insects with names bigger than they were. In the Great Hall, people threw bones and gristle on the floor, where the dogs were always on hand. And they brought their own retinue of insects.

Europeans were also filthy and did not bathe more than two or three times a year. They seemed to think perfumes and powders were an adequate substitute for water. Even the most well-bred thought nothing of wiping his nose with his hand and then shoving that same hand into a dish of mutton stew. He recalled once telling Lord Bertrand that the Italians ate with a device called a fork. Lord Bertrand had scoffed and said, "God would not have given us fingers if He hadn't intended us to use them to eat with."

Then there was the matter of his color.

Even after all these years, there were unexpected moments when his awareness of his black skin was as sharp and painful as the burning of scalding water. Such moments were less predictable than the advent of a storm. One moment he resided securely in his body. The next he felt outside, a disembodied spirit looking at a lone black man amid a desert of whiteness. No one looking at him would have known of this shift in his vision, this unwanted and sudden consciousness of self and difference. At that moment, anyone looking at him would have seen him leaning to his left, appearing to listen avidly to Lord Bertrand, nodding his head, and now offering his own words.

"Though I saw the King just a few days ago, my lord, I cannot tell you the reason for his visit here. However, I cannot believe it could portend anything but good."

No one could see the agitation in the soul of the black man, an agitation even he did not understand. How had he come to be sitting in the Great Hall of Lord Bertrand's castle surrounded by people as pale as fog who thought he was one of them?

Couldn't they see that was not so? Did they not notice how silent he became when they spoke of their childhoods? Their memories were not his. Without a lifetime of shared memories, how could he belong to them? How could they know him?

He was an illusion and illusions could not eat pheasant breast and mutton. If he were a charade he would have sated his thirst with duplicity, not grog and mead and wine. Suddenly, almost desperately, he tore at the pheasant with his fingers and stuffed the moist white meat into his mouth. *I am real,* he told himself. *See. I am chewing the flesh of the fowl. My teeth grind it into a wet paste and now, see, I swallow.* He raised a bowl of red wine to his lips and emptied it without pausing for breath.

As he finished, he was startled by loud shouting and stomping of feet.

"Hail, Othello!" someone cried.

"Hail, Othello!" everyone in the Great Hall shouted in response.

"More wine for Othello!" another voice shouted.

"More wine for Othello!" the throng repeated.

Quickly a serving girl hurried forward with a pitcher of wine and refilled the bowl beside Othello.

Othello stood up, raised the bowl, his face stretched wide with an open grin. "To England!" he shouted.

"To England!" came the roaring response.

Othello drank and all followed.

"To the King!" he shouted.

Everyone leaped to their feet. "The King! The King!"

They raised their bowls and drank.

Othello resumed his seat. His fingers tore another chunk of flesh from the pheasant's breast. He shoved it into his mouth and chewed noisily. He was all right now. Perhaps he was only tired. Yes, that was it! He was merely tired. Nothing more.

"Ah!" Lord Bertrand exclaimed.

Othello looked up. There, at the far end of the hall, stood Desdemona in a long dress of black velvet. It was cut low and cinched tightly at the waist. Her pale skin gleamed with the brightness of the crescent moon. Her dark hair spilled over her shoulders like silken desire.

As she walked slowly toward the head table, everyone quieted, and she seemed to savor the attention her entrance caused. Lord Bertrand watched with the pride and bewilderment of a father unable to understand how his daughter had come into the ways of a woman. And what was he to do about it? What *could* he do? If he had had his way she would have been married by now. He was in danger of being a laughing-stock if she were not married within the year.

Where had she gotten the notion that she must be in love with the man she married? Love had nothing to do with marriage. He had not loved her mother in the beginning. Love was not something that happened all at once. It grew slowly and in silence, as the leaf within the limb forms even while frost sheaths the twig. He feared she mistook a quickening of the pulse, loss of self-recognition, and a warming in the loins for love.

He would have to arrange a marriage, which he should have done while she was yet a child. Her marriage to the Duke of Leceister's young-est son would please the King. He would speak frankly to her when the King came. Marriage was too sensitive a matter to be left to a flooded heart. As for love, well, if it did not come in time with the one to whom you were wed, you looked elsewhere. At least that was so if you were the husband. However, he could also name a few wives who had done the same. The man who allowed such a wife to live was not honored for his permissiveness.

As Desdemona mounted the platform, Lord Bertrand and Othello rose. They bowed and she curtsied modestly in response. Lord Bertrand gestured toward the chair on the other side of his.

Desdemona smiled. "Here, Father. Why don't you sit there and let me sit between you and the General. I am eager to hear all that has transpired since he led the men off to battle."

Lord Bertrand good-naturedly allowed his daughter to have her way. When all were again seated, Desdemona looked at Othello and said, "It is good to see that my lord has returned safely."

Othello chuckled. "The Duke of Leceister decided peace was red-blooded."

Lord Bertrand laughed. "Indeed! That robber took one look at your black face and knew he would be seeing his own red blood soon enough if he did not become enamored of peace."

"Not so, my Lord," Othello responded uneasily, not sure how to respond to Lord Bertrand's allusion to his color. "I fear my reputation for fierceness exceeds my deeds."

"And is it now my turn to say, 'Not so, my lord'?" Desdemona interrupted.

"What do you mean?" Othello asked her.

"Have you not heard the stories about the

black giant, Othello, who is afraid of nothing, not even the Angel of Death?"

"Do not believe such stories. A soldier who is not afraid of death will kill when killing is not required. I would not be such a man, nor have such a one under my command. A true soldier loves life and wants as much of it for his enemy as for himself."

"Well spoken, Othello," Lord Bertrand interjected. "Well spoken. However, what is that tale I've heard about you in Spain?"

"Ah, that! Well, though I want life for my enemy, I did not say I wanted my enemy to have life at the expense of my own. It was an unfortunate incident. In brief I found myself at an inn at Toledo. My size, my sun-scorched flesh made me an object of curiosity to some soldiers who had had too much wine. There have been some who think to prove their manhood by reducing my girth to a corpse. They do not think that a man of my size can also move as quickly as lightning between clouds. They do not see that with only one of my hands I can encircle the necks of all but the stoutest men, and with that one hand I can snap their necks or squeeze until they die. On that day they sought also to do that which they should not to Emily. I remember the look of death on each and every face."

"What does it feel like to kill a man?" Desdemona asked innocently.

Othello was silent for a moment. "At first there is a satisfaction. You are alive and he who would have had you dead is not. There is relief that the danger is past and exaltation that you yet remain alive. Afterwards, however, maybe hours later, sometimes, days or weeks later, there comes a sadness, a melancholy even, an emptiness in the spirit that I cannot explain. There are nights when someone I have killed will come to me in my sleep and gaze at me with such mournfulness that I awaken, my face wet with tears."

Desdemona was careful not to look at him, afraid she would not restrain herself from covering his furrowed brow with kisses and letting his tears flow onto her breasts.

"But it has been some years since I have killed a man. And I will probably never do so again. The armies of the future will use guns and rifles and kill men with the fire of powder and metal. It will be possible to kill a man without looking into his face. That is not my idea of a soldier."

"You sound as if you are ready to retire from the business of war," Desdemona offered.

"I might consider it if there were a compelling reason," he said, looking directly at her.

Desdemona blushed. "And what would the King do without you?"

Othello laughed. "No man is irreplaceable."

"But there is only one Othello," Lord Bertrand put in. "And the King knows it."

The conversation moved to less personal matters as Lord Bertrand prattled about the preparations necessary for the King's impending visit. Neither Othello nor Desdemona listened closely. They sat quietly, the tension of thoughts and feelings unexpressed linking them as intimately as touch of lips upon lips. Neither dared look on the other for fear that look would become embrace and embrace ignite the seasoned wood of passion.

Finally, Lord Bertrand's stream of words dried and there was a sudden silence. Desdemona rushed to fill it as if it were a threatened breach in a dike.

"A moment ago when my lord Othello was relating his frightening story of the fight in Spain, he mentioned there were men threatening Emily. How long have you known her, my lord?"

Grateful for the offering of a topic, Othello rushed to answer. "Many years. I was already a man when the Mandinkas attacked our village. They took us by surprise. Before we could defend ourselves we were taken captive. The one you know as Iago and I were sold to Berbers and taken north to Algerine where we were made to serve in the household of a wealthy merchant. There among the girls who waited on him was one of wide eyes mournful enough to make a skylark weep. Iago fell in love with her the instant he saw her. They were both children. She could not have been more than twelve. I suppose Iago was around sixteen. I am the closest either of them has ever had to a father. When I escaped some four years later, I could not leave them behind."

"I fear that my lord is depriving us of the tale of another adventure," Desdemona chided.

"You must forgive my daughter," Lord Bertrand interrupted. "She has always had a weakness for a tale, be it true or false. She prizes a well-made tale more than she does a husband, I fear."

"Perhaps, Father, I merely await a husband who can make a tale."

"Is that not what I said?" her father rejoined.

Desdemona wanted to look at Othello to see if he had understood her words. Her father had not. She was glad men could be so dense. But surely Othello had heard.

She rose from the table. "It is getting late."

Lord Bertrand and Othello stood up.

Othello bowed and, taking her hand, kissed it with lips a little too moist for courtesy's requirements, which lingered an instant longer than ritual needed. He squeezed her hand enough for the pressure to be unmistakable and released it. "Until the next tale," he said softly, looking directly into her eyes.

Flustered, Desdemona curtsied awkwardly and hurried from the hall.

Chapter Four

Iago

Iago looked down from the gatehouse tower as Othello rode over the drawbridge, Michael Cassio riding next to him. A servant with a torch led the way.

"There goes our new lieutenant," whispered an ingratiating voice.

"Indeed, Richard. Indeed."

The two men watched the torch as it bobbed and bounced in the darkness like a child's fears. Soon the light was scarcely a blemish on the blackness of night as the riders disappeared, turned off the avenue and onto the path that led through the trees to the manor house Lord Bertrand had made available to Othello.

Iago knew what Othello did not suspect: Lord Bertrand despised him for his black skin. Iago knew because he made it his business to find the hidden lusts and hatreds that men nurtured like a mother holding a baby to her breast.

Iago's appearance belied his constantly observing mind. Almost as tall as Othello and as black of skin, he appeared more soft than powerful. Perhaps it was the absence of a beard, but he appeared open where Othello's beard-wreathed face gave his mien a martial sternness. Iago's face seemed always to be smiling and this invited others to take him into their confidence. His blackness was soon forgotten. That was how he learned Lord Bertrand despised Othello.

One evening some months ago, an evening like this one, only colder, Iago was standing watch. Lord Bertrand, unable to sleep, came up to the keep. They chatted without aim for some moments when Lord Bertrand offered, "It is a pity that Othello is not more like you, Iago."

"My lord?"

"Don't misunderstand me. I am grateful to Othello for his military prowess but I do not trust the man himself. Not as I trust you. There is something about him that does not permit one to overlook his blackness. You present yourself as a man like any of us. With Othello, I don't know. Perhaps it is the way he carries himself. Even the King feels intimidated by him. You, sir, despite your skin color, are no different from any English nobleman. You play a good game of cards, are not averse to having a little fun with one of the serving girls, can drink as much wine and ale as any two men, and know more good jokes than the King's jester. But Othello does none of those things. He does not give one the opportunity to forget his blackness."

"I am not certain my lord does Othello justice. But, be that as it may, I would be remiss if I did not thank you for your good opinion of me. I am flattered to be thought of so highly by one such as you."

"Think nothing of it. Your skin may be black but your soul's as white as any man's, and that's what counts."

Iago had kept his face as blank as a cloudless sky and his manner as languid as a spring morning. People had a strange tendency to equate silence with agreement. So when Lord Bertrand yawned, gave Iago a slap on the back, and went to bed, he could not have guessed how insulted Iago had been by his words.

Iago made certain no one ever knew what he was thinking even as they were convinced he was taking them into the innermost chambers of his confidence. Of anyone he supposed Richard knew him best, which meant scarcely at all rather than not at all.

Iago and Othello were in the service of the Duke of Mantua in Italy a short time after coming to Europe those many years ago. In one of the bloodiest battles he had ever fought in, they had laid waste to a village. The Duke had given orders that nothing and no one should remain, not even an olive tree. So it was. Except for a boy about ten. Iago had found Richard in the cellar of a burning house, hiding in a tun of wine. Afterwards Iago wondered if he would have killed him if he had been hiding in an empty cask. To hide in the wine itself revealed a will to survive that Iago admired.

He had been a boy when the Mandinkas came and burned their village. Iago had heard his father scream with pain. He had heard his father sob. He had smelled it when his father lost control of his bowels. And he had been ashamed. He had never told anyone — not Enaharo, not Ashaki. But he had never forgotten.

Othello had found Iago hiding in the bush. For some days the two eluded the Mandinkas before being captured and sold North. It was then Iago learned: Who you were did not matter. Survival depended on appearing to be what others wanted you to be. That was all anyone cared about.

Iago had no doubt that had they remained among the Musselmen of the North, he would have converted and eventually become a caliph. They had liked him enormously and had admired how quickly he learned Arabic. He would have stayed — if not for Ashaki.

He and Othello had been slaves in the household of a wealthy merchant in Oran. Othello's size and demeanor had made him a natural to be the merchant's personal protector.

Though Iago was of equal size, no one thought him fit for war. When the merchant discovered his gift of words, he was trained as a secretary. One morning during the first months in his new capacity, a slave girl with eyes as round as sorrow came in to serve coffee. Iago loved her from that moment.

Later that day he was crossing the courtyard. He saw Othello and the girl in conversation.

They squatted on the ground in the shadows outside the women's quarters. As he came closer he saw smiles in both their eyes. Adoration caused her face to shine with the majesty of a full moon. In that instant a hatred for Othello was born that nothing, not even his eventual marriage to Ashaki, would expunge. Instead he waited for her face to shine with polished desire when she looked at *him*. It never had.

"So, what do you think of our new lieutenant?"

Richard's voice brought him back. "You know as well as I, as all the men know, that he does not deserve the promotion."

"What will you do about it?"

"Do?" Iago wondered. He started to protest that he could do nothing, but who or what said so? In all these years it had not occurred to him that he could *do* anything about the dissatisfactions that kept his innards tied in knots. But what if he could? What if he could not only reduce Michael Cassio in rank but reduce also the one who had promoted him?

"Let us watch and wait," he said to Richard. "Opportunity comes to the cat who lies as if asleep."

Chapter Five

Othello Speaks with Michael Cassio

"A sip of ale or wine, Michael Cassio," Othello offered.

"No, General. I do not drink."

Othello laughed. "A soldier who does not drink? That is like saying a soldier who does not fight."

"I know, but too close a friendship with spirits causes the spirits of beasts to take over my own. I assure you, General, it is not a sight that would delight or amuse you."

"You know best."

Othello pointed to the bench at the crude table before the fireplace. Michael sat. Othello sat opposite him.

"You saw her?" he asked abruptly.

"I did, sir."

"And? Do you enjoy making me feel like a man about to be hanged? What does she say?"

"I have known Desdemona all my life, sir, and never have I seen her more radiant. She loves you."

Othello sighed. "If I could believe that, I would be so wealthy the King with all his coffers would be a pauper next to me."

"All she could speak of was you."

"What should I do next, Michael Cassio? I know nothing of love. My tongue turns to bone in my mouth when I think of speaking of my love to her."

"I will be your tongue, sir."

"If you would do that for me, Michael Cassio, I would be in your debt forever."

"And I free you of any such indebtedness. I do it not only for you whom I admire and respect, but for her who is as dear to me as a sister. What do you want her to know?"

"Two things gnaw at my innards. There is gray in this beard. Much more gray is to come. That is one worry.

"The other is more basic. While I might shave my beard to keep the gray from being seen, there is no remedy for my blackness. I am no fool. I know there are many who disdain me for my blackness. That disdain would be extended to her.

"Tell her I understand if, on reflection, she should decide that one such as I am would be too great a burden. She is young and beautiful with skin as white as Christ's soul. Any man could be hers. There is no reason she should choose me."

Michael rose. "Though I know what she will say, I will speak with her as early in the morning as I can."

"And you will come to me soon thereafter?"

"With haste."

Othello stood and shook the young man's hand firmly. "Thank you, Michael Cassio. Regardless of the outcome, you have earned my heart's gratitude."

Chapter Six

Michael's Regrets

With the arrival of the King that morning, no one noticed the frequent trips Michael Cassio was making between the castle and Othello's manor house. No one, except Iago from his post on the battlement.

He had been there since sunrise, had watched the fog disentangle itself from the hills, though scraps like pieces of torn nightgowns remained in the valleys for some time. He had come to attention when he heard the castle gates open and an instant later the slow, muffled sound of horses' hooves. Who would be riding out while the grass blades were still bowed with heavy dew?

"Lieutenant Cassio!" he said with soft sarcasm. Why was he about, riding slowly as if care must be taken that no one hear or see? Iago had heard that Cassio had a girl by the name of Belinda, if memory served. But love's time was darkness when touch replaced sight and sighs were an orator's tongue. And a man eager to see his woman rode as if he would create winds to replace those engendered by the Almighty. Cassio rode slowly as if by so doing, he would never reach his destination.

Iago did not like questions without answers. Where another man would have shrugged, Iago was not so casual. Perhaps he would never discover the answer, but it was certain he would not forget the question.

For his part, Michael Cassio would be glad when the next sun rose. It would be over then. One would have thought it a simple task to carry messages. But a message was more than words. It was tone of voice, nuance of expression, the softness of the eyes, and where love was concerned, he thought now that the words had nothing to do with the message at all.

He rode slowly because he wanted time to understand why he no longer relished his role as messenger for the two would-be lovers. But there was no great mystery, was there?

Despite his repeated assertions of any but brotherly feelings for Desdemona, he had merely said what she wanted to hear. But he had always assumed a day would come when she would look at him and see — a man who loved her.

His life's deepest regret would be that he had played the charade of friend and never told her. But could love speak of itself if it was not certain it would be heard, if it feared it would be mocked, laughed at, and dismissed? Or did love need to be spoken and make even the deaf to hear? Love was not timid, and that had been his error. He had lacked the courage of his love.

Now it was too late. He rode to the village to bring Father Thomas to the castle to offer mass for the King. During the course of the ride from village to castle, Michael would tell the priest that late in the night he was to go to the chapel and wait. A couple who wished to be joined in holy matrimony would be brought to him. Michael would mention no names because Father Thomas was not known for an ability to keep a secret. More than one person had heard from another an account of transgressions they had thought were locked in the secrecy of the priest's soul. It was not that Father Thomas was malicious. Quite the contrary. A bee's honey was not as sweet. He simply loved gossip and his job brought more to his ears than anyone's in the realm. People had had to learn which sins to confess and which to leave until the Day of Judgment.

Knowing Father Thomas would be tempted to go from the marriage ceremony to Lord Bertrand's chamber, Michael would not give the priest an opportunity to yield but would return him to the village that night.

And what would he, Michael Cassio, do then?

Chapter Seven

Othello and Desdemona

He raised his hand to knock at the door. At that instant the door opened.

"My lord," Desdemona said, her voice barely audible, eyes cast downward. She stepped back, opening the door wide.

Othello entered with slow, almost halting movement as if by so doing, time would adjust itself to his pace and each moment last a year, each year a decade, and a decade an eternity.

Desdemona closed the door softly. Now that she was alone with him, now that he was there in her chamber, all the boldness of imagined passion had fled. She was as silent as that hour of deepest night when even Death, fearing itself, hesitates to walk abroad.

Though she could not have known it, her fear and inability to look at him called forth feelings in Othello he had not known since saving Ashaki from being made part of the merchant's harem, a story only he and she shared. But those had been feelings whose promise offered no opportunity for fulfillment. He had seen how Modibo looked at her. Even if he had not known of Modibo's feelings, he would not have made Ashaki his wife. Every love does not require consummation or even touch. He had been wise enough to know that.

He knew he had been right because now, he wrapped Desdemona in his arms and held her as if she were part of himself that had been lost and, only after he stopped searching, found.

Her head lay on his chest as if she rested from a wandering journey which, to that moment, she had not known she had been on. Enclosed in his arms she could feel the strength in his body. It was far greater than his size portended. It was not so much a physical power, though that was there, as the power of one who commands life and death. With a twist of the wrist, a thrusting of the arm, men — how many? — had gone from life's promise to death's inviolable security. She pressed her cheek even more into his chest as if wanting to feel his blood-churning heart against her face.

For the longest while they did not speak. They did not move. In the stillness and the quiet each became aware of the other's beating heart. Each felt the other's breath as it made its journey from the caverns of the lungs, up through the trachea, and out at the nostrils. Soon, it was not clear whose heart beat behind which breast, whose breath was expelled from which nostrils.

"I have something for you," he whispered finally.

He gave her a handkerchief as red as sunset. "It is not a jewel that would make you the envy of all the women of London. It is not an exotic perfume. It is far more. Guard it with your very life. If you do, there is no happiness that will not be yours."

Desdemona took the handkerchief and held it across her hands as if it were the finest silk spun by worms in the gardens of the Emperor of Cathay. "Thank you, my lord." She folded it and placed it inside her dress, between her breasts. "There. It will always be next to my heart — where only your hand may touch."

He took her to him again, this time bending to kiss her lips with a touch as soft as a rose's petal.

"I have done nothing to be worthy of such a one as you. I could do nothing to be worthy of you. If you will accept that I will always try and I will always fail to reach a state of worthiness, I would be honored if you would be my wife."

Desdemona blushed. "It is I who am unworthy, my lord. Only your desire that I be your wife redeems me."

He kissed her again, this time more firmly but still with the gentleness of an infant's breath.

"The priest will come here at the first hour after the midnight watch. I will come moments after. We will become one for all eternity."

"My heart awaits your return because it will not beat again until you do."

Another soft kiss and he was gone.

❖ ❖ ❖

It was long past the time he and every God-fearing man should have been in bed. Father Thomas sat in the darkness of the dim candle-light of the chapel and yawned loudly. He was beginning to regret he had ever promised Michael Cassio that he would perform this wedding. Young Cassio was so secretive, too, not telling the priest whom he would be marrying. The more he thought about it, the more Father Thomas didn't like it. Whoever the couple was, why couldn't they marry in daylight where God and man could smile on them?

Father Thomas had his suspicions. Obviously Cassio was the groom. That meant the bride was none other than Lord Bertrand's young daughter, Desdemona. It was a union Father Thomas approved of and hoped he would not have to suffer Lord Bertrand's wrath for sanctifying it secretly.

Just as the priest was beginning to grow impatient, the chapel door opened. Desdemona walked in, followed by Michael Cassio, who closed the door. When Father Thomas saw her, the qualms he had been harboring in his chest like thieves eager to steal one's hard-earned joys were banished. Who would have thought Michael Cassio could put such love in a woman's face? Desdemona was radiant with the promise of union, and for an instant, Father Thomas regretted that no woman's face had ever nor would ever flame with passion at the thought of him. Nor his at the thought of any woman.

More young people were insisting on marrying

those whom they loved. He did not wholly understand. But neither did he entirely disapprove. He had reminded angry parents that God Himself was Love. If two young people found themselves bound one to the other by well-twined strands of love, how could he not ask the blessing of He who was Love beyond all imagining?

"My lady," he greeted Desdemona, bowing.

"Father," she returned, with a hurried curtsy.

"Michael," he smiled warmly at Cassio.

"Father."

"Before we begin, might I say a word or two?" the priest asked. Without waiting for a response, Father Thomas continued, not noticing the embarrassment on Michael's face and the confusion on Desdemona's. "I can understand your eagerness. Passion is not patient and seeks its fulfillment even if it consumes those who would fulfill it. But don't you think it best that Lord Bertrand be informed? I know he would be shocked at first. Maybe even a little angry. But give him a day or two and he would have the biggest celebration the castle and village have ever known. Quite frankly I am uneasy about the prospects of any marriage born when darkness shines as fiercely as light of day. Michael Cassio. From the look I see on Desdemona's face, I have no doubt that she will love you even more two or three days from now as she does this night."

"Your intent runs ahead of your knowledge,

Father," Michael responded. "The one responsible for the love in her heart is not yet here."

"I beg your pardon. You mean, I am not to marry the two of you?"

"That would be almost like incest," Desdemona said. "Michael is loved too deeply like a brother for there to be the passion of husband and wife between us."

"Then who?"

Just then there was a soft rapping at the door. Michael opened it.

When Father Thomas saw the large black man walk in, he wondered what had brought him here. Then the priest looked at Desdemona. Her entire being was fixed on the black man as if she were an arrow and he the bull's-eye of the target she would penetrate at its exact center.

Desdemona flung herself into Othello's arms.

"My love! My one sweet love!" she said with a wholeness of soul any man would have died to have had said to him.

Othello held her tightly. "My precious one!"

Father Thomas was sorry now he had not followed that instinct that told him to find his way from the castle and to his house in the village. Satan was riding earlier than usual this night. Lord Bertrand would want his head once he learned that the priest had married his daughter to a black man.

There were two black men at the castle, but Father Thomas had never bothered to meet them or learn one from the other. He had seen this one at the banquet earlier that evening sitting next to the King. He must be Othello, the King's mercenary who would kill anyone for the right amount of gold.

Perhaps even a village priest! Damn you, Michael Cassio! May your soul dance for eternity among the flames of hell!

A sheen of perspiration glistened on the priest's balding skull as he thought quickly of how to extricate himself from this situation. The answer came almost immediately. Love could be unhorsed if the bridle has not been properly placed, he thought, congratulating himself.

Father Thomas cleared his throat ostentatiously. Othello and Desdemona broke their embrace.

"Forgive us, Father," Othello said. "Passion seeks its own course without the grace of sacrament."

"Yes, yes. Well, I'm glad you mentioned sacrament. I cannot perform this wedding."

"Why? What's wrong?" Desdemona asked, suddenly afraid.

The priest turned to her, finding it easier to speak with her than to the fearful blackness. "Obviously, your intended comes from another country and clime, one where, unfortunately, the souls are damned to burn in hell because they have not received the sacraments of the Church, or worse, they worship false gods. I would be excommunicated if I wed you to a heathen."

Othello laughed. "I thought you might indulge in such musings. I was baptized in the kingdom of Naples a decade ago. Here!" From a pouch at his waist he brought out a folded piece of paper and handed it to Father Thomas. "My certificate of baptism."

Father Thomas examined it carefully. Without doubt it was genuine. He had no excuse now. Fear, anxiety, and foreboding were not legitimate reasons, he knew, but that did not make them any less real — or true.

He returned the paper to Othello. "I am certain you can understand my caution."

Othello wondered if Father Thomas would have been as diligent in his ecclesiastical responsibilities if Desdemona's husband-to-be had had white skin. "May we begin now?" he said to the priest.

❖ ❖ ❖

Desdemona.

Her name was as warm and soft as the arched blackness of night.

Desdemona.

If he had known love would make him attentive to every mote in creation, he would have exchanged his sword for it years ago. But was this something he could have known with anyone but her? No.

Desdemona.

It had been a year since the King had sent him north to train Lord Bertrand's men in the ways of war. He and Modibo set to work shaping the Lord's men into soldiers. Ashaki had become lady-in-waiting to Lord Bertrand's daughter.

Desdemona.

He had heard her name first on a cold winter day when the wind blew in from the sea with the sound of death cries. They were gathered in the Great Hall, drinking heated wine and ale against the cold, with nothing to do until the storm passed. Some of the men played cards, while others rolled dice, and most simply talked and joked. The loneliness of each man rubbed against that of the other but if the two pains rubbed long enough and hard enough, a companionship grew between them and sometimes that was enough to make it from one day to the next.

Othello knew it well, having seen it among soldiers in Italy and Spain and France and now here. He knew it for them as well as for himself. A soldier plunged into battle not because he was brave or knew or cared about what he fought for. What was risk of death compared to unrelieved and unwanted solitude?

He wondered now if he had not seen her before that day or simply not noticed her. Or perhaps the day before she had been a child still. No matter how gradual and subtle the transformation of girl to woman, there had to be one day, and yes, even a moment in that day, when the woman subdued the girl and was seen for the first time. Perhaps that was the moment he raised his eyes and saw Desdemona entering the Great Hall.

He thought he had never seen a woman more beautiful. It was not the mysterious combination of form and shape of lips, nose, eyes, cheeks, and shape of head that made a face appealing or ugly. Beauty was created by the dance of the animated soul in the body. In all his years and all his travels, Othello had never seen so much life wanting to be contained by and yet free of one body.

Now she was his.

They rode slowly through the forest. There was no need for a torch as the horse knew the way as surely as morning knew the sun. They rode silently, not having exchanged a word since Father Thomas had made them husband and wife. There were no words for a love that felt as new as the day just beginning and as old as the stars. There were no words for the cessation of loneliness and the consequent completion now his.

Yet there was also an uneasiness, a disquietude that gnawed at him. What if something happened to her? Who would he be then? The nature of love was that only with and through a particular other could you become who you truly were.

They rode through the darkness to the manor house, one heart beating, one breath breathing.

Chapter Eight

Lord Bertrand Hears the News

When Iago heard hooves clatter over the drawbridge, he looked down. In the light of the torches on either side of the castle gate, he saw Michael Cassio astride a horse. Behind him sat the priest from the village, holding a small torch.

Strange. What was the priest doing up so long past his bedtime? And why would Michael Cassio risk the road down the mountain at this hour? It was a precarious ride in daylight. Even with the King and his entourage in attendance, there had to have been a spare room somewhere in the castle the priest could have used for the night.

The numbers did not add up to any sum Iago could understand. What was so important that a priest was needed until this hour? Was someone ill, dying, and the priest was needed to hear their final confession? What else would keep the priest at the castle until near the close of the second watch? My God! Had the King taken ill? Was the King dead? God forbid! Without the King's support, he and Othello might be seeking employment from some other sovereign.

Iago was so engrossed in his own reflections at what he had surmised to be the death of the King that he almost didn't hear the sound of the second horse. In fact, it was Richard who said, "Do you see what I see?"

Iago recognized Othello moving the horse slowly, and almost without a sound, off the drawbridge and onto the avenue. Behind him, her arms as tightly around his waist as a well-made wedding band on a bride's finger, was Desdemona.

"Well, well, well," Iago whispered to himself. "I believe Enaharo has given me the rope by which to hang him. Priests not only do the last rites. They also perform marriages, even ones that would outrage God and man if performed in the light of the sun."

Iago supposed he might have forgiven Enaharo for holding Ashaki's heart for all these years. But this? Marriage to a white woman? A white woman was to be used for whatever pleasure she might bring, but to love, to marry? Never! Better to be as celibate as a priest. Now Enaharo would never want to return to Africa. Iago could not bear the prospect of spending the rest of his life amid Europe's whiteness.

No white man would ever conceive that he was loathsome to a black, not for any deeds he may have committed, but purely as a physical being — the pasty skin like dough that refused to be leavened, the lank and thin strands of hair in unnatural colors, the noses as keen as lance points, the lips as thin as a knife's edge. They were an ugly sight to behold.

Enaharo had now become one. Finally, Iago had the passion to destroy him.

He debated leaving his post to awaken Lord Bertrand. But would he make himself liable for reprimand by leaving his post when there was no danger? And Othello and Desdemona could be easily found.

He began to plot his course. When he went to Lord Bertrand he had to be careful to appear the loyal servant placing his allegiance to the Crown above fealty to his friend. However, it was crucial also that he not appear to be a tattler, but merely one doing his duty. He had to make it appear, though, that death would have been more welcome.

Iago had no doubt Lord Bertrand would take advantage of the King's presence and demand justice. Although the King was fond of Othello, Iago was willing to wager the King was more fond of his whiteness. He would not be pleased to imagine black lips and white ones joined.

❖ ❖ ❖

The rapping at the door of his chamber was so soft Lord Bertrand was uncertain he had heard anything at all.

"Do you hear something?" he asked James, his servant.

"The door, sir?"

"It's probably one of the King's men with some outlandish request. Hurry to it."

Lord Bertrand slipped into his velvet robe. While a visit from the King was flattering and did nothing to hurt his standing in the realm, it was also quite stressful. If any need of the King's was not anticipated, Lord Bertrand could find himself out of favor.

"It is Iago, sir," James said when he returned.

"Iago?" Lord Bertrand asked, not recognizing the name.

"The other black man."

"Can't he wait until he sees me in the Great Hall? I have to attend to the King."

"That is what I suggested to him, sir. He agreed, but hinted that if he waited for a more opportune moment he feared your wrath that he had not sought you out sooner."

Lord Bertrand nodded. "Very well. Bring him in. No. I'll go out. I don't think I want that negro smell in my inner chambers. I might never be able to get it out."

Iago stood waiting in the anteroom, wondering why Lord Bertrand had not bothered to lower his voice, or did he not know his voice carried like a cow bell across a meadow? Perhaps Lord Bertrand did not believe a black man would hear anything a white man did not want him to hear.

"What can I do for you?" Lord Bertrand said. "This had better be important."

"That is for you to determine, my lord. However, it is not what you can do for me, but what I, perhaps, can do for you."

"Speak and be quick about it. I must attend on the King."

Iago hesitated. "Then, perhaps I should come back later. Yes, perhaps that is what I should do. After all, whether you learn of it now or later this morning or early this evening will change nothing. What's done is done."

"Very well. Out with it, but hurry!" Lord Bertrand snapped.

"Your daughter."

"Desdemona? Has some accident befallen her? Is she dead? Do not tell me that she is dead."

"No, my lord, but you might wish her so."

"Has she fallen into a deep sleep, then, from which no one can awake her, and yet she lives?"

"She has fallen into the lair of a great beast."

"Well, don't just stand there. Let us call up the men and search the woods."

"It is not that kind of beast, my lord."

"My God, man! Will you stop speaking in riddles and say it out plain!"

Iago smiled wryly. "I want nothing more than to do that, my lord. However, there have been too many instances in history when the messenger has been faulted for his message and paid the price. I do not want such a fate to befall me."

"You have my word. Now, speak! What is it with my Desdemona?"

"Very well. Let me pose a question. Have you ever considered what it would be like if the King were to visit in a year and you present to him a grandchild as sooty as coal?"

"Are you telling me that you have gotten my daughter with child?" he roared.

Iago chuckled. "Forgive me. I can see how my clumsy words would be open to such misinterpretation. No, my lord. I prefer my women both older and, forgive me, more possessed of the color of the earth. However, you are close to the mark." He paused and then, almost with pleasure, said, "Your daughter and Othello were married by the village priest this very night."

Lord Bertrand turned red, spluttered, and then yelled, "You lie!"

"On occasion I believe we all do," Iago returned quietly, "but this is not one. Send to her room and see if she is there. Then send to the manor house and see if she is there."

Lord Bertrand ordered James to go down the hallway to Desdemona's chamber and bring her to him. James returned a moment later. "The black speaks at least half the truth, my lord. Desdemona is not in her room."

Lord Bertrand blanched. "Gather some men, Iago. We must rescue her from the one who stole her in the night."

Iago cleared his throat. "Begging your pardon, sir. Perhaps my observations are in error, but is not Othello an especial favorite of the King?

Would it reflect badly on his lordship for him to take action against Othello when the King himself is present?"

Lord Bertrand looked at Iago, and after a moment, nodded. "What would you suggest?"

"Inform the King. Let him act on your behalf."

Lord Bertrand smiled. "You will tell the King what you have told me."

"If you wish," he said without enthusiasm.

"I wish."

Chapter Nine

Iago Pays a Visit

"And how did you sleep, my love?" Desdemona asked when Othello awakened that morning.

"With the peace of the soldier who knows he will never have to draw a sword again. And you?"

"I did not. I could not. I lay awake to guard your breathing, to implore your heart to continue its beating for many years to come. I would have you live forever."

Othello smiled. "And I shall — for you."

Never had anyone looked at him with eyes so filled with awe. He doubted that the Pope adored his God as fervently as Desdemona adored him. Never had he been important in anyone's life. Ashaki and Modibo would mourn his passing, but their lives were not dependent on his as if he were sun and they planets.

For a moment he wished he could elude those blue eyes that gazed on him as if he were her newborn child. It was a terrifying responsibility to receive her soul and let it rest in the palm of his trembling hand. More terrifying was knowing his soul lay like a feather in the palm of hers. If she were to cease to love him, he could not exist. He did not like that feeling. He did not like this loss of control that love demanded. Could he go into battle now as fearlessly as he had before she took his soul? Would he look now into the face of an enemy and see there love of a beloved that was twin to his own love? Could he kill a man who was loved as he was, who loved as he did? Othello refused to answer. Perhaps he would never have to. Hopefully this day would need eternity to unfold.

He pressed her hand to his lips. "I did not know that love could make a man feel both weak and strong. I did not know I could feel so alive and yet so afraid of life. How could one who has held the power of life and death over so many men now be ready to fall upon his sword if you should ask me, would plunge a dagger into his heart without hesitation should you leave me?"

"We will have no talk of death on such a morning. Don't you see, my lord? In our love death has met its match. Death will one day end our lives, but never our love."

He pulled her to him and they became one breath in one heart.

❖ ❖ ❖

Later that morning they were sitting at the table eating when there was a knock at the door. Othello and Desdemona exchanged amused glances. Her absence from the castle had been discovered.

The peasant woman who attended Othello

and did the cooking started toward the door, but Othello motioned her away and went to the door himself. He expected to see an irate Lord Bertrand on the other side. Instead there stood a smiling Iago.

"Modibo," Othello whispered with delight.

Iago laughed. "Enaharo."

The two men embraced, and Othello led the younger man inside.

"So what brings you here?" Othello asked with a knowing chuckle.

"The King thought you would be more receptive to the light in my eyes than the blood in Lord Bertrand's." He bowed to Desdemona. "Congratulations, my lady. My wife and I are delighted for you and for Othello. His happiness means much to us. I know you will bring him much."

"Thank you, Iago."

"So, tell us. What is the news from the castle?" Othello motioned for Iago to take a seat on the bench and Othello sat down opposite, next to Desdemona.

"Well, I suppose it was when Desdemona failed to appear for breakfast." He turned to look at her. "I thank you for keeping Ashaki ignorant of your plans. When Lord Bertrand questioned her, she was able in all honesty to say she knew nothing. She is quite inept at dissimulating, I fear. At any rate, Lord Bertrand was beside himself with anxiety. He feared you had been kidnapped until he questioned the men who were on watch last night. One of them reported seeing Michael Cassio returning the priest to the village at a time when wolves are more comfortable than men. Cassio was brought forward and after threatening him with the dungeon, he confessed he had arranged for the two of you to be married and that you were now here.

"I will spare you a description of Lord Bertrand's rage. He turned so red many of us feared the blood would burst from his body and speckle us all. He was ready to call up the men and have them march here and reclaim his daughter. He is convinced that you used some magical potion from darkest Africa to bewitch Desdemona. That Desdemona is here of her own free will is a notion he is incapable of entertaining.

"In any event, I doubted that the men would take arms against their general. I did not want to risk the potential embarrassment and loss of face Lord Bertrand would suffer if the men refused to obey him."

"That was quick and wise thinking on your part," Othello put in. "I can't tell you how much it means that I have always been able to count on you."

"Your words honor me too much. I did nothing exceptional. I merely suggested to his lordship that since you were in the King's service, how fortunate that the King is here. This is a matter the King might wish to resolve himself since it involved the general the King had come to rely on most. Lord Bertrand saw immediately that my words bespoke a modicum of common sense. He requested and was granted an immediate audience with the King. The King was kind enough to ask me my opinion. I said that you had no intention to hide or deceive, and if the King requested your presence and an explanation you would come without hesitation."

"Well spoken. Well spoken. Even without a summons from the King we would have appeared at the castle for dinner this evening."

"That will be fine, I'm sure. It will give time for Lord Bertrand's temper to cool."

Desdemona shook her head. "No. My father will use the hours to blow on the coals to keep them at white heat."

"Lord Bertrand seems to be especially talented at making matters difficult. How is the King disposed?" Othello asked.

Iago paused for a minute. "Of that I am not sure. You have put him in a difficult position. On the one hand, he needs you. On the other, he needs Lord Bertrand's loyalty, not to mention taxes. The King will do what is in the King's interest."

Othello nodded. "Just so. Thank you for your intervention. Without your loyalty and quick thinking, the situation would be out of hand by now."

The two men stood and walked toward the door.

"Please send my regards to Emily," Desdemona called. "Tell her that I am more happy than I dreamed was possible."

Iago bowed. "It will please her to hear that."

Othello and Iago hugged, and the younger man was off.

Chapter Ten

The King Remembers

The King would have preferred Lord Bertrand to handle his own affairs. But no marriage was a strictly personal matter. He sometimes wished otherwise. Not that life with Elaine had been bad. Neither of them would have married the other if it had not been arranged, but things had turned out better than could have been expected. They were civil with each other, and even shared measured portions of affection from time to time.

But when told of last night's event, he had been saddened by an unexpected envy. Othello and Desdemona had acted on their passion. What was that like? he wondered. How did it feel to do something because it mattered to you? That was why he liked the African. Othello was able to forget himself in passion.

What if? No question was more cruel. What if?

The last time he had been here at the castle was to attend her funeral. But she was not supposed to have died yet. The messenger came with her letter one evening. The King had left at dawn the following morning.

Willingham Castle
11 June 15 —

Your Highness,

At the time of my mother's final illness, I recall her saying how odd it was that only at the end of life did you learn what was important. Death's nearness made it imperative to uncover whatever meaning there had been, to know what had been vital in your life before losing it forever. I asked what that had been for her. Flowers, she said. As you know, we had the most magnificent flower and herb gardens. I often wished my mother had given me the care and attention she gave her garden. She knew: Do not think I loved you less than my garden, she said. I loved you more because I had it.

Now that my time is near I envy my mother anew. She had what she loved most. I did not.

Nothing ever mattered in my life but you. Now, when it is too late, <u>I realize this was what was important and where my life's meaning lay.</u> I never stopped loving you, not for an instant. I have lived each day of all these years imagining I am with you. I do not imagine myself as your Queen. I would *have been content to be your mistress. Were we too noble for passion? Did we choose safety? Love cannot be love if it is cautious. Love mocks Death. In the presence of love Death relents. When Death came for my mother, it placed a smile at the corners of her lips. It will not place one at mine.*

I hope Desdemona will not be afraid of passion, will not subsume passion's requirements for those of civilization. We were too civilized, you and I. We did our parents' bidding and I married Bertrand, and you, Elaine. Each is a nice person, but did you ever awaken in the morning looking forward to seeing Elaine? Did you ever feel your heart expand with gladness from love for her?

Before I die, I want to see your face again and feel your lips on mine.

Julia

Though he rode from sun to sun, he could travel only fifteen miles a day. It had taken the messenger seven days to reach him. She died on the morning of the sixth day of his journey to her. He arrived in the afternoon.

Lord Bertrand had been surprised to see him. He had not known that his wife and the King had been childhood friends. If not for grief he might have wondered why his wife would have kept such important information secret. But Lord Bertrand was not a devious man or a very bright one and thought nothing of the King's request to be alone with the body.

When the King saw her lying in the bed, he realized that he never stopped loving her, either. She had been wise enough to live with the grief for a love that could not be fulfilled. He loved her even more because she had suffered love's absence rather than live a lie.

And he? He lacked even the passion to have lived a lie. He was the King. He had issued decrees, fought wars, fathered children, legitimate and otherwise, intrigued against this one and executed that one. But he had failed to love. Failing that, he had not lived in his life.

Chapter Eleven

Lord Bertrand Fights for His Daughter

As the time drew near to plead his case before the King, Lord Bertrand wondered if he had not erred in bringing the matter to the King's attention. Would it have not been wiser to have said nothing, waiting until the King departed, *then* ordered Othello to leave? The news would not have reached the King for a week. Another week, if not more, would have passed before the King could have gotten word back to him to do nothing to Othello. By that time the African would have gone off and been difficult to find. And by that time, Desdemona would have been freed from whatever spell the black demon had cast over her.

But if he had dared dismiss Othello, who, after all, was in the employ of the King, the King might have taken Lord Bertrand's head.

No, this was the best course. He had no doubt his eloquence would prevail over that of the African, whose eloquence was limited to the sword. The King would probably decide the marriage should be annulled. He would have to find someplace else to station Othello, perhaps at the Duke of Leceister's. Lord Bertrand hoped this episode would help the King see the risks in paying blacks to protect England. When there was no one to fight, the blacks would not make themselves invisible, though the devils had the power to do that. No, they would want to sleep in English beds with English women. The next thing anyone knew English men would have grandchildren who were neither white nor black. That was against nature.

There was a knock at the door of Lord Bertrand's chamber. A page told him that Othello had arrived and the King awaited both of them in the Great Hall.

Lord Bertrand nodded, took several deep breaths, then hurried down the stairwell, along the corridor, and into the Great Hall. He paused when he saw the King sitting in his chair. On either side sat the King's councillor, the Duke of Widdington; the Exchequer, Lord Russell; and various others of the King's court. He had expected a smaller gathering, one that would have permitted more intimate conversation, and he could have subtly reminded the King of their long friendship as well as the King's affection for his now-departed wife. However, he was uncertain what tone to adopt before the King and all his advisors.

Othello stood at the far end of the room. Seated on the bench at the table next to him was Desdemona. When Lord Bertrand saw how his daughter looked up at the African as if she had been robbed of all will and intelligence, any hesitance about what he should say or how he should say it fled.

"Gentlemen." The resonant voice of the King's councillor filled the room. "Lord Bertrand. General."

Lord Bertrand and Othello moved to the front of the hall. Lord Bertrand stood at a distance from Othello who, it seemed to him, was unnaturally relaxed for a man so guilty.

"I believe that you, my Lord, requested the King's wisdom in this matter."

"That is so, your Lordship."

"State your case."

Lord Bertrand cleared his throat. "Your Highness. I am grateful you have agreed to take of your time to render a decision in this matter. I would not have brought it to your attention if it were only a personal matter. However, I perceive in this affair a potential threat to the Crown itself."

"That is quite a charge," the King interrupted. "Are you accusing Othello of treason?"

"No, Your Highness. Not treason in the sense that a man would take up arms and seek to overthrow the Crown. I have no reason to question the General's loyalty to you — if a mercenary can be loyal to any but his own interests."

Lord Russell, the Exchequer, laughed in his high-pitched voice. "That argument will avail you nothing, Lord Bertrand. You wouldn't know, of course, but at the same time the General received an offer from our King, he also entertained offers from Spain and France. Those offers would have paid him more money. The General accepted the King's offer. By that alone he earned our trust."

Lord Bertrand flushed red at the reprimand but refused to accede. "Even so, it is no secret to you or anyone that I have always opposed the use of mercenaries of any kind. But that is neither here nor there. The King asked me if I were, accusing the General of treason. I am not. However, treason is not the only way the Crown could be threatened."

He paused and looked toward the back of the hall where Desdemona sat. "Threats to the Crown can be direct — an attempted assassination — God preserve the King. Threats can be indirect and subtle. That is why the King has many advisors, men whose task it is to keep their eyes and ears open in order to see and hear the tiniest dropping of a stone into a pond, the ripples of which can disturb the tranquil surface.

"The King has known my daughter, the fair Desdemona, since she was born. From the beginning her mother and I assumed that when the time came, her marriage would do much to enhance the power of the King. The time arrived. Young men from across the realm came to court her, young men of wealth and standing. They came courting with poems and flowers and music. A woman would have been proud to be married to any one of them. Indeed, I believe one was your youngest son, Lord Russell.

"Though I was growing impatient for my daughter to make a decision, I was not overly concerned. This is a new age and I try to keep up with the times. Our parents told us whom we were to marry, made all the arrangements, and we were expected to be there at the appointed hour or die under our father's sword." There was an appreciative chuckle from the men on the platform. "Today, our children talk of love, and we allow them more latitude than we were allowed. But all understand that when the time comes, it might be necessary to make other arrangements if the one you love does not correspond to the one your parents love." There was louder laughter.

"And then *this* came!" Lord Bertrand shouted suddenly, pointing to Othello as if his arm were an arrow shot from a bow. "I fear I am not as vigilant as the King's advisors who can identify a threat while it still appears benign. I noticed no interest between Othello and my daughter. I invited Othello to sit with me at meals, at the very table where you now sit, Your Highness, my daughter between us. They chatted but there was nothing unusual in that. I heard no sighs from her of what the young people call love. In his tone I detected none of the leer we men know how to do with our voices as well as our eyes." The men laughed warmly in affectionate recognition.

"Now, I ask myself if I am a fool. I knew nothing until this very morning when my daughter did not appear for breakfast. It was then I learned she was married in the dead of night to *this!*" Again the arm shot out at Othello.

"Your Highness. My Lords. I ask you. Why would a loving and fair daughter have her wedding in the bowl of the night? I ask you, why would a daughter not invite her own father to her wedding? I ask you, why would a daughter not even tell her father she was going to marry?" He stopped and walked slowly over to Othello. "But, even more, Your Highness, my Lords, I ask you this: Is it not the custom in our land that the man who seeks to marry one of our fair daughters presents himself before that daughter's father and gains permission? Is that not what each of us did before we married our wives? Even the King presented himself like a suitor before the father of she who became our Queen. Perhaps in other lands, the customs are different. I know not the habits of those who live where the sun blackens the skin and coarsens the hair. But *here* where God and the King rule, we do not take other men's daughters in the night."

There was a stirring as the King's advisors whispered with each other in accord with Lord Bertrand's last statements.

Encouraged, Lord Bertrand continued. "All this day I have asked myself, why? Why would my daughter deceive me, her father, and marry in this shameful manner? I have been able to come up with only one answer. You have enchanted her!" he shouted into Othello's face. "Damned as you are by your black skin, you have cast a spell on her and taken from her the will to think, the ability to see. Why else would a girl so tender, fair, and happy, a girl who was not eager to marry, a girl who turned away the wealthiest and most handsome men of the realm, including the son of the King's own treasurer, why, I ask you, would a girl turn her back on her upbringing and her own people and run to the sooty bosom of such a thing as you? You have violated her with drugs and spells from the jungles of your cursed land. Left to itself, Nature would not mix black and white and could not, except for some kind of witchcraft."

Lord Bertrand was known throughout the realm for his outbursts of rage, but no one had ever seen him this angry. Blood had rushed to his face, turning it a deep red, and his body was as rigid as a sword.

Throughout the tirade, Othello's benign expression had remained unchanged. Some of the King's men would have sworn they had seen the corners of his mouth turn up in amusement. Even if that was not certain, they were all impressed that he had maintained his calm. Each of them knew he would have killed any man for saying half such things about them.

As Lord Bertrand looked into the placid eyes of the African, something told him that he had lost already. Othello looked on him as serenely as the full moon. Lord Bertrand did not know how to withdraw without losing face, and he was grateful when Othello, sensing his embarrassment, moved toward the platform and began speaking.

"Your Highness. Your Lordships. I am at a disadvantage here because I am not a man of words. Even when I was young and dwelled among my people and spoke only the tongue in which I was raised, I was not known as one for whom words flowed as smoothly as water over stones. Now I am called upon to defend my honor and to do so in a tongue not my own. I hope the King and his Lordships will keep this in mind as I try to explain.

"There is no magic here except that which love creates. There is no witchcraft here except that which love casts upon the hearts of lover and beloved. The only drug here is love itself. It casts spells no witch could produce even if he had at his disposal all the evil herbs and potions in the world.

"You gentlemen are more learned than I. You have studied the ancient thinkers and philosophers. I am not learned or a thinker, but I have been told that even Plato and Socrates and Aristotle could not explain love. If they did not understand, who is Lord Bertrand to think he can?"

"Hear! Hear!" one of the King's men agreed loudly.

"Since coming to reside here I have taken my meals at the very table where you now sit, and each day I have been honored to sit next to Lord

Bertrand. Many times he has asked me to tell him of my travels through the lands of the Arabs, my journeys in Turkey, Italy, and Portugal and Spain and France. He seemed especially curious to hear of my homeland.

"So I told him stories about the ancient rulers of my country. There was Kanissa'ai, a King of Ghana of old. He had one thousand horses and each horse had a mattress to sleep on, three servants to attend it, and its own urinal made of copper."

The King and his men laughed uproariously.

When the laughing subsided, Othello continued. "In the evening, it was Kanissa'ai's custom to come out of his palace to talk with the people. A thousand faggots would be lighted and he would sit on a balcony made of gold and, the stories say, the balconies gleamed red in the fire-light.

"There was another King of Ghana who would sit in a pavilion surrounded by ten horses whose bridles and bits and reins were embroidered from gold. Behind the King ten pages would stand holding shields and gold-mounted swords. To the King's right would stand the princes of the empire with gold plaited in their hair."

The King and his men interrupted with laughter again, trying to imagine what each of them would look like with gold in his hair. Lord Bertrand stood to the side and glowered.

Finally the laughter subsided and Othello was permitted to continue. "And I told Lord Bertrand of the great Mansa Musa of the kingdom of Mali. It is said that when Mansa Musa made his pilgrimage to Mecca, the holy city of the Muslims, he was accompanied by 60,000 men and that each man carried a bar of gold weighing four pounds. And when Mansa Musa addressed anyone in his kingdom, they bowed and sprinkled their heads with dust."

"I like that!" the King exclaimed, laughing. "I will issue a decree immediately ordering all of you to sprinkle your heads with dust whenever I speak to you." He laughed loudly. "But most of you would sooner kill yourselves than dirty your perfumed locks."

His men chuckled uncomfortably.

"And I wonder if that would be a loss," he muttered softly, but loudly enough for all to hear. "Go on, my General."

"I told him of some of the strange customs in the countries where I have sojourned. He was shocked to learn that not only the women but the men of France wear earrings and that the Italians eat with an instrument called a fork rather than with their fingers. I will not bore you with more such detail, but wanted to give you an idea of the kinds of things that were talked about at the table.

"Lord Bertrand did not notice how eagerly Desdemona listened to my tales. But I could see her face, and I saw there how her imagination was fired by what she heard. She would look at me with a mixture of admiration and even awe.

When I would relate my tales of the battles in which I have engaged, when I would describe the times I have come close to death, my heart would almost break from the look of sympathy and concern I saw on her face.

"Love is a language whose alphabet I never learned. Another man would have seen clearly what was happening. It took me a while to understand my eagerness to see her at meals, my delight in looking on her face and hearing her voice. It took me a while to understand that I was in love. It took even longer to recognize her love of me." Othello turned toward Lord Bertrand. "It pains me, my lord, to hear your true opinion of me. I counted you as friend. I did not know you went from sitting next to me at meals to disparaging my color when I left the room. It was not I who made me as black as night that all men must respect. My color was of your God's choosing. If you have a disagreement, address it to Him."

"Hear, hear!" the King's men murmured.

"I love Desdemona, my lord. If my passion was the sun, it would scorch the earth, leaving nothing but cold cinders." He turned and looked at her. "The most painful death would be as nothing compared to the death I would feel if she were to love another, or die. I had not loved before her. I can never love another. She is my life. How could I not make her my wife?"

There was a long silence. Finally, the Duke of Widdington spoke. "You do yourself an injus-

tice, General, when you say you are not a man
of words. After listening to you, and imagining
the stories you must have related in Lady Desdemona's hearing, I think we can all count ourselves fortunate that our wives have not had the
opportunity to listen to you." The men chuckled. "I daresay, I will see to it that my own wife
will never have the opportunity. While women
admire men of action, there are but few who
will not succumb to a man who knows how to
direct words to her heart. The only magic used
here, Lord Bertrand, was that of language. All of
us know the power of the word to elevate us
above the clouds or bring us to the depths of
hell."

"Well spoken, councillor," the King said.
"Lord Bertrand, your son-in-law is far more fair than
black. I see no evidence of witchcraft or chicanery
here."

Lord Bertrand tried to contain his anger. "Your
Highness, I do not believe my daughter would
fall in love with what she feared to look at."

"May I be permitted to speak?" came the soft
but firm voice of Desdemona from the back of
the hall.

"I wish you would," said the King. "Come
forward."

Desdemona stood before her father and took
his hand. "It pains me that you should be so
grieved at my happiness, Father. How strange
that tears should be in both our eyes. Yet the
salt in yours burns while the salt in mine is a

seasoning. You would fault me because I look on him and am enchanted and not repulsed? You would fault me that I care to know the mysteries of that black skin and would have him marvel at mine? You would fault me that these red lips would kiss the black scars from his battles? You would fault me that he, who has lived most of his life as a stranger in strange lands, has found a home in me? You would fault me that I have found my purpose in being that home for him? Mother would be as ashamed of you as I am, Father."

If the King had had any remaining questions, her last remark would have removed them. He was almost overcome with the emptiness Julia's death had created in him, an emptiness that seemed to expand the longer she was in the grave. Looking down at Desdemona he saw her mother when she was young — the same blue eyes and dark hair — but more, the determination in the eyes, the ferocity of the heart's conviction. That was what he envied about the African. He believed his heart. That was a luxury kings could not afford, but it was one that kings were duty bound to encourage.

The King rose. "Lord Bertrand. As a father I share the concerns and distress that we as parents must withstand. In this case, however, I see no cause for concern or distress. He loves her. She loves him. Would that every man and woman married to each other could say the same."

Lord Bertrand bowed. "Yes, Your Majesty. May I make one request then?"

"Speak."

"It was Your Majesty's pleasure that the African live at my estate. I would ask Your Majesty to find another's estate for him and my daughter."

The King frowned. "You would separate yourself from your only child?"

"I have no child."

"You have a child. It is clear-sightedness you lack. If this is your wish a year from now, I will grant it. But give yourself time to let your temper moderate."

"Your wish is my command, sire, but you do not understand. What child would so deceive her father? I do not know the child that would do such." Lord Bertrand turned toward Othello, who stood holding Desdemona's hand. "And you, sir, be careful. She deceived her father. She will deceive you."

Chapter Twelve

Iago Begins His Plot

Usually the Great Hall was noisy. Soldiers were not known for decorum or manners. Whatever they did, they did loudly and with a fullness of spirit permitted only to those who have learned in their marrow that Death is always as close as the next heartbeat.

This evening, though, the men were quiet. The place at the head table where the General always sat looking down at them was empty. In fact, no one sat there. The men had heard rumors but most of them knew only that the Lady Desdemona had married their general and Lord Bertrand was displeased.

Iago sat in a corner of the Great Hall. "You would think someone had died," he said to Richard.

"I suppose if you were Lord Bertrand, someone has."

Iago smiled. "Well spoken. But this moroseness is not good for the morale of the troops. What if we were suddenly called to arms?"

"Why, the mood of the men would change immediately."

"Perhaps. But is it not the job of the lieutenant

to ensure that the men are always ready for arms? Isn't it the job of the lieutenant to see that the men's swords are always polished and their spirits high?"

"I see your point."

"And where is our lieutenant?"

The two surveyed the hall. "Ah! There!" said Richard.

"Where?"

"At the table to the left of the platform."

"Ah, yes," Iago said. "And who is the woman who engages his interest more than duty?"

"Belinda."

"And she and Cassio are, shall we say, involved?"

"Oh, quite."

"I see," Iago murmured to himself. "Richard. I have a task for you."

"With pleasure, sir."

"Among the King's men there is one Charles of Paddington. He is a stout fellow. He is easy to find because he has taken up the new and disgusting custom of smoking tobacco. The awful smell will lead you to him. Ask him if he has any whiskey."

"Whiskey? Isn't that the new drink strong enough to make a man forget his name and where he was born?"

"Indeed. Wouldn't you think it appropriate for our lieutenant to show his elation at the marriage of our general by offering a toast or two with a sip of whiskey?"

Richard smiled and left quickly.

Iago made his way slowly toward the front of the hall. As he went he stopped at each table to exchange pleasantries with the men. He intimated that a drink or two in honor of their general's marriage might not be inappropriate. Having a legitimate excuse for serious drinking cheered the men immediately.

"Good evening, Lieutenant," Iago greeted Michael Cassio when he reached the front table.

"Iago. A good evening to you."

Iago looked pointedly at the young woman sitting next to him.

"Ah, this is Belinda."

The young woman bowed her head to Iago.

"A very handsome couple you make," Iago said.

"Thank you, sir," Belinda replied.

"It is I who should thank you for the pleasure you bring to my eyes."

Michael laughed. "Your eloquence is unbounded this evening."

"In point of fact, it is your eloquence I have come to make use of."

"I fear you now seek to make a fool of me."

"Not at all. Not at all. I have been speaking with the men. They feel somewhat left out of the momentous event that took place last night. It is not every day their general gets married, and it is certainly not every day a general as famed as our Othello marries. They asked me to inquire if you would lead them in a toast for Othello and the Lady Desdemona?"

Michael shook his head. "I forget myself if I drink spirits, even a glass. Not only would you not recognize me, I do not recognize myself. You are far more eloquent, Iago, and can withstand spirits far better."

"But I am not their lieutenant," Iago said without a trace of rancor. "And, I think the men need to see you as being more like them, if you know what I mean. You are young and untested. They will, of course, obey you because the General has made you the second-in-command, but it is not certain that they will respect you."

Just then Richard returned with a jug. Iago spotted him, waved his arm, and Richard came over to the table.

"Here's the very thing," Iago said, taking the jug. "It's a new drink called whiskey. It is all the rage in London, I understand. Why don't we fill a couple of cups for the men to pass around and we'll get one for you. Who knows? Perhaps whiskey will agree with you where wine and beer have not?"

"If I had known being second-in-command would require this much, I would have declined." Michael sighed. "As you wish."

Cups were quickly procured, the whiskey poured, and the men quieted. Michael Cassio stood before them nervously. He cleared his throat several times. "I thought it would be appropriate for us to raise a toast to the General and his new bride."

"Hear, hear!" the men shouted back.

"To General Othello and Lady Desdemona. May they have a hundred years of happiness."

"A hundred years!" everyone roared in agreement.

He raised his cup of whiskey, and not knowing any better, took in a large mouthful as if it were water. But instead of his tongue and throat finding a cool smoothness, it was as if he had ingested liquid fire. He gagged and coughed, his eyes bulging as the liquor burned its way through his system. The men, seeing his distress, began laughing at him.

Iago feigned concern and pounded Michael on the back. "Here. Take another sip. It will help clear your system."

Michael did so, this time taking only a small sip. It did seem to help clear the passages, though it burned his innards hotter than the sun on the plains of Spain.

"To the General!" he shouted boisterously, a feathery lightness exploding in his brain.

"The General!" the men called.

And they drank.

"To Lady Desdemona!"

"Lady Desdemona!'

They drank again.

"To the King!"

All the men leaped to their feet.

"The King! The King!"
"The King!"
"The King! The King!"
Iago could not believe that Michael had become inebriated so quickly. But to a body unaccustomed to the gentle warming of beer and wine and ale, whiskey was stronger than the intoxicating weeds they smoked in the north of Africa.

Iago moved quietly over to where Richard stood watching in amazement the transformation in Michael. "What do you suppose Othello would do if his lieutenant was to be involved in a drunken brawl!" he whispered.

Richard looked at Iago, not understanding at first. Then, he smiled and nodded. The men were singing now:

> "And let me the canakin clink, clink;
> And let me the canakin clink:
>   A soldier's a man;
>   A life's but a span;
> So please let a soldier drink."

Iago moved slowly among the men patting this one and that one on the back until he saw William, a man whom it was rumored had studied for the priesthood but had left or been kicked out. No one knew for sure and no one cared enough to ask. There was not a braver man among them, except the General. There had been more than one battle that had been swung in their favor by the mere sight of William and the General standing side by side, their swords flashing in the sunlight.

"Good Iago!"

"William."

"Is it not almost time for the Lieutenant to set the evening watch?" William asked.

"Indeed, it is. Despite his lack of experience, he is a soldier fit to stand by Caesar. Yet his vice is the same length as his virtue like shadow and sunlight at the moment of the equinox. What a pity. It makes me fearful to think of the trust Othello puts in him."

"Is he like this often?"

"Each night this is how he induces."

"The General should be apprised of this. He sees Cassio through the eyes of his own good nature."

Just then there came a loud shout from the front of the room.

"I'm not drunk, I tell you!" came the slurred voice of Michael Cassio.

Iago could see that Richard had his hands on Michael's shoulders as if trying to lead him from the hall.

"If you don't take your hands off me, I'll beat you into a wicker bottle."

"This is distressing," William said to Iago. "Should not we send for the General?"

"I fear you may be right."

"It is a pity to have to disturb a man so newly wed."

"He and Lady Desdemona have not departed for the manor as yet. I believe they are in her chamber packing her belongings."

"I'll make haste there."

There was a loud commotion as Michael Cassio pushed Richard onto a table, and leaping on him, put his hands at his throat. Richard grabbed Michael's wrists and pushed until the pressure against his throat was eased. Iago and several other men moved forward quickly and pulled Michael from Richard.

"Is there a problem, Lieutenant?" he said softly.

"Ah, Iago! Problem? No. None at all. Your friend accused me of being drunk, which everyone can plainly see is a lie!" Michael answered, breathing hard, his face flushed and sweaty from the sudden exertion.

"Obviously. But perhaps we could sit down. For some reason you seem to have attracted the attention of all the men."

Michael looked around the hall to see the men staring at him. Their gazes were bereft of respect for the authority of their second-in-command. Instead, he saw expressions of disgust and contempt. Suddenly ashamed, he allowed Iago to lead him to a bench where he sat down beside Belinda.

"What happened?" he asked her. "Have I made a fool of myself?"

Before she could respond, their attention was drawn by the sound of hurrying footsteps on the stone stairs leading from the upper chambers of the castle down to the Great Hall. In a moment Othello swept into the room followed by William. The men leaped to their feet.

"What goes on here?" Othello demanded to know, looking around.

No one answered.

Othello went to Michael Cassio, who lowered his head.

"What goes on here, Lieutenant?" Othello asked.

Michael did not answer.

Othello looked at Iago.

Iago looked away. "I do not know," he said quietly. "Frankly, I wish I had lost the legs that brought me here."

"William? It is you who brought me here. What goes on?"

"Perhaps I overreacted, General. What I saw I saw only from a distance and perhaps my eyes deceived me. Iago knows more than I and it was he who sent me to you."

Othello was beginning to be angry. "Iago! Speak! That is an order!"

Iago shook his head. "I would rather have this tongue cut from my mouth than to have it do offense to Michael Cassio. Yet, I persuade myself that nothing shall wrong him if I speak the truth. I was at the back of the hall speaking with William when I heard a shout from this part of the room. I looked and the Lieutenant was arguing with Richard about something. I believe I heard Michael Cassio say he was not drunk and he would fight any man who said he was."

"Drunk!" Othello exclaimed.

"He had had the merest sip of whiskey to lead the men in a toast to your recent nuptials. It was scarcely enough to wet the tongue. And even if it had been more, can one really blame a man for excesses in celebrating your marriage?"

"If that man is my second-in-command, I can and will blame him."

"I don't think that will be necessary. I daresay that any one of us here would grow angry if we were falsely accused of drunkenness while on duty. Under such circumstances even I would pull a knife on or choke the life out of any man."

"I know that you seek to make this matter light on Cassio, and that is to your credit. Michael Cassio, I love you but you are no longer my officer." Before Cassio could respond, Othello turned and addressed the men. "Why sit you here? Is it not time for the night watch? Be about your duties!" Othello left the hall and the men followed quickly.

Iago looked at Belinda, who sat with an arm around Michael's slumped shoulders. With his eyes he indicated that he wanted her to leave. She hesitated, then kissed Michael on the cheek and left.

"You sit as if you were a wealthy man who has just learned he has lost all his fortune."

"I have, Iago, I have. I have lost my reputation. I

have lost the immortal part of myself, and what remains is bestial."

"I thought you had lost something of substance, like gold and jewels. Reputation is often got without merit and lost without deserving. You have not lost your reputation unless you make yourself such a loser. You can regain your previous standing with the General."

"I don't think that will be possible."

"What happened between you and Richard? Did he provoke you?"

Michael shook his head. "I don't remember anything distinctly."

"Well, it is of no moment. The General knows that any man may be drunk and do deeds he could not imagine while sober. This is what you should do. Our general's wife is now the general. When a man marries his judgments soften and his focus changes. His wife's opinion now matters more than the King's decrees. Go to Desdemona. Confess yourself freely to her; ask her to help put you in your place again. She is of so free, so kind, so blessed a disposition. Indeed, she thinks it a vice in her goodness not to do more than is asked of her. Ask her to make a splint for this broken bone between you and her husband. I would wager you that if she does, this crack of your love shall grow stronger than it was before."

"Thank you for these good words of advice, and thank you for seeking to defend me before the General."

"You need not thank me."

"What would I do without a friend such as you. I will go to Desdemona tomorrow and plead my case."

"And you will succeed, for you are in the right. Good night, Lieutenant."

"Good night, Iago."

Iago watched Michael leave the hall. Matters were proceeding more easily than he could have anticipated. So quickly had Cassio been demoted. Bringing down a general might not be so difficult after all. He knew Enaharo well. His heart's life had beat to the clang of sword and that graying of the light in a man's eyes when he knew he was not wounded but dying. Enaharo knew as little of women and their ways as a pig knew of Aristotle. It would not be difficult to make Enaharo believe that when Desdemona pleaded with him on Michael Cassio's behalf, the appeal was not as innocent as it might sound. And who would Enaharo believe? When all was said and done, you trusted those who knew you as instinctively as a bird knew how to sing. Whenever Modibo spoke with Enaharo in the tongue of their childhood, Modibo could hear the older man's soul longing for that comfort which comes only when one is known by another even when he is silent. Modibo knew Enaharo's loneliness because it was also his. But Enaharo did not know his own loneliness. Modibo would use Desdemona's goodness and make the net that would enmesh them all.

Iago's revery was broken by Richard slipping into the hall.

"And how goes it, Richard?"

Richard looked around to make sure they were alone. "Michael Cassio pulled no knife on me," he said quietly.

Iago's eyes narrowed. "Go on."

Richard looked around again. "What do you suppose the General would think if he learned that what he saw was not as real as he thought? What I know would make the General change his opinion and his judgment about Cassio — and others."

"Do you mean to say that the seals on your silence may leak if they are not fortified with gold?"

"I do not know of a mercenary in the King's service who ever became wealthy just being a mercenary."

"And you would like to be wealthy?"

"No, no. Do not misunderstand me. I seek not wealth. Merely a little more than I have now."

Iago smiled. "You're a good man, Richard. I trust a man who thinks of his own interests and looks after them. However, I am disappointed you thought you needed to blackmail me. Once this affair is concluded, I was going to show my appreciation for your invaluable services in the manner you have indicated. I am disappointed you did not surmise that on your own."

Richard blushed, embarrassed. "Please forgive

me. If I had thought, of course I would have known. I did not think. Forgive me. Please forget I was here. Good night. Good night." He hurried from the hall.

Frowning, Iago watched him scurry out, then went swiftly through the narrow winding halls of the castle to his room.

"Ashaki," he said softly, when he entered.

Emily smiled. "Modibo."

"How is the new bride?" he wanted to know.

"Well, considering. She was not expecting to have to choose between her father and her husband. But, having done so, she is at peace. She loves Enaharo."

"And does he love her?"

Ashaki looked at her husband. "With all his soul. Do you doubt it?"

"No. That is how it appears to me, but women have a keener sense of these things. If the glow of his love were destined to die like an ember in the fireplace, you would have perceived it. Did you hear the news about young Lieutenant Cassio?"

"Michael? No. What happened?"

"Well, the men decided to have a few drinks to celebrate Enaharo's wedding. Cassio thought he could drink down whiskey as if it were spring water. Before anyone knew it, he was drunk and spoiling for a fight. Richard tried to get him to go to his quarters and sleep it off. The next thing anyone knew, Cassio had struck Richard and lay astride him, a knife at his throat."

"No!"

"I was able to wrestle Cassio away before the blade descended."

"Thank God you were there!"

"Indeed. Unfortunately for Cassio, someone sent for Enaharo and when he learned what had happened, he stripped Cassio of his rank."

"Poor Michael! Being divested of his rank does not hurt him as much as losing Enaharo's respect."

"Well, if you are willing, I think we can help him regain both."

"How?"

"I told Cassio to ask Desdemona to take his case to her husband. What newly married man can refuse his bride?"

Ashaki laughed. "Unlike those men who have been married for a while."

"And what have I ever refused you?"

"And what have I ever asked?" she countered. "I decided I would live more happily if I avoided the pain of being refused."

Iago looked at her sharply, surprised by the truth of her insight.

"But, forgive me," Ashaki continued, her voice lighter. "What can I do to help Michael?"

"Will you see Desdemona tomorrow?"

"Of course. There is much more packing to be done. She will be here at the castle in the morning."

"Good. Do you think you could arrange to have her in her mother's garden, oh, when the sun is midway between dawn and the zenith?"

"I don't see why I can't arrange that."

"Good. I'll have young Cassio come to the garden at that time to make his case."

"I like your plan, Modibo. We'll have Michael a lieutenant again in no time."

Chapter Thirteen

Michael Cassio Pleads with Desdemona

Since her mother's death, Desdemona came to the castle garden often. Its six large beds of flowers were laid with geometrical precision in squares and bordered on all sides by walkways — camomile like small suns with their yellow centers and white petals; lilac-blue penny-royal; pink-petaled daisies; purple, yellow, and white violets; yellow cowslip; and red and white rose campion. At the end of the central walk, poised on a rise, was the gazebo where her mother would sit and watch the servants tend the garden.

When Emily had suggested they break from packing and go to the garden, Desdemona was eager. Moving from the castle meant giving up the garden. Though there was a smaller and quite lovely one back of the manor house, there were no memories of her mother in that garden. Now, she was going to be without her father, too. The knowledge brought sadness but one free of self-pity.

"Is there ever gain without loss?" she asked Emily, who sat beside her on the bench in the gazebo.

"Why do you ask?"

"It was something that occurred to me last night when I began packing and again this morning. I have gained a husband and lost a father and a home."

"I do not know if there can be gain without loss, but there can be loss without gain."

Emily was staring into space and Desdemona wondered if she was seeing the home and parents she had been taken from as a child. Was she seeing all the years and all the places she had been since? Desdemona thought it would be exciting to travel over Africa and Europe. There was no excitement on Emily's face, only the pain of a loss she had never expressed, a pain for which there were no words or screams or tears vast enough.

"I wonder if my father will gain anything from his loss?"

"I did not know your father so hated black people."

"Nor I. He hid it well. It causes me to wonder now what other feelings he has hidden from me, from us all." She was about to say more when she saw a figure coming. "Is that not Michael?"

"I believe it is."

A few moments later Michael Cassio entered the gazebo and bowed. After the three exchanged greetings, Desdemona asked, "And what brings you here? Surely you can't be bringing me a message." She laughed at the memory of Michael's role in her courtship.

"How I wish those days would return."

"What do you mean?"

"Last evening I sought to make a toast with the men in celebration of your marriage. I drank too much or too quickly. Before I knew it, I was drunk and engaged in a brawl. I have been stripped of my rank and lost Othello's respect."

"Oh, I am so sorry," Desdemona commiserated. "I will speak to Othello and all will be as it was. He will not long hold this offense against you."

"If you do this for me, I will be your faithful servant for the rest of my life."

"Well, I know you love my lord. It is not right that the two men in my life should be as strangers to each other. Do not despair. I was forced to choose between my father and my husband. My wounds are still fresh with the blood of rejection and exile. Mine are for life, it seems, but I'll not see you bleed so long."

"I believe I see Othello and my husband coming this way."

Michael and Desdemona looked up to see Othello and Iago far enough away to make out their forms, though not their faces.

"I must go before they arrive," Michael said.

"No. Stay and hear me speak on your behalf."

He shook his head. "I am ashamed to be in the General's presence."

"Then go. But do not despair. I'll have this matter settled in no time."

Chapter Fourteen

Iago Plants Seeds

"I don't like that," Iago said quietly as he and Othello walked toward the garden where their wives sat.

"What's that?"

"Oh, nothing. Or something, but I don't know what."

"Isn't that Michael Cassio leaving the garden?" Othello asked as he saw a figure moving rapidly away.

"Cassio? I doubt it. I wouldn't think that he would steal away so guilty-like, seeing you coming."

"Nevertheless, I think it was he," Othello said as if posing a question to himself, though there was no question mark in his voice.

A brooding silence surrounded the two men as they entered the garden.

Desdemona kissed Othello lightly on the lips. "I was just speaking with someone who languishes in your displeasure," she said.

"Oh. And who would that be?"

"Michael, your lieutenant at this time yesterday, a mere soldier today. I beg of you, my lord, if I have any grace or power to move you, restore him to his rank of yesterday."

"Was that he I saw leaving here just now?"

"Yes, it was, but I fear he left part of his grief with me and I do suffer with him. You can call him back right now."

Othello was amused and annoyed. In his country a woman would not have intruded herself into a man's affairs. Here it seemed more custom than exception. "I'll see to the matter some other time."

"What other time?" she wanted to know.

He wanted to be angry with her but the innocence and guilelessness of her face soothed his ire. "As soon as I can."

"Does that mean at supper tonight?"

"No, not tonight."

"Tomorrow at dinner, then."

"I will be with the men at that time."

"Please let it be soon. Michael is truly penitent for what happened last night. Any man is deserving to be forgiven one error. And, do not forget, my lord, this is the same Michael Cassio who carried messages of love between you and me, and on more than one occasion when I had doubts, it was Michael Cassio who spoke your part."

Othello nodded, smiling at the memory of his recent courtship. "How can I deny you anything? Enough. I will restore him to his rank but not just yet. It would not be seemly for a general to change his mind so quickly."

Desdemona gave a squeal of delight and hugged him. "Thank you, my lord. Come, Emily. We have been away from the packing long enough." She turned to go, then stopped, and looked back. "Oh, I hope you don't mind. I asked Emily to tend to our needs at the manor house. The old woman who cooked and cleaned for you was not very good at either, you know."

Othello roared with laughter. "It will be a pleasure to have Emily around more." As the two women walked away, Othello looked longingly after his wife. "Oh, how I love you," he whispered softly. "And should I ever cease loving you, chaos is come again."

Iago cleared his throat. "Enaharo."

"Ah, forgive me, Modibo. There was something you wanted to discuss with me. We have gotten distracted. What is on your mind?"

"Ironically, I, too, had planned to raise with you the matter of Cassio's demotion. But did I understand your wife to say that Michael Cassio knew of your love and acted in your behalf?"

"That is so. Why do you ask?"

Iago shook his head. "No reason. I just wanted to satisfy a thought I had."

"And what thought was that?"

"I knew they had been childhood friends but I was not aware they were still close."

"I hadn't thought about it, but I suppose they are."

"Indeed!"

"Indeed?" Othello repeated. "Is there something the matter? Is there some dishonesty in Cassio of which I am unaware?"

"Dishonesty, Enaharo?"

"Dishonesty! Yes, dishonesty!"

Iago shrugged. "For all I know he is as honest as the next man."

"Well, what do you think?"

"What do I think?"

"Why do you mock me with an echo?" Othello burst out. "You talk as if there is some monster in your thought too hideous for me to see. Is there something going on that I should know about yet no one wants me to know about it? Why, only a few moments ago you said you didn't like it when we saw Cassio leaving my wife. Yet, you would not tell me what it was you didn't like. And, just now when I told you that he served as a messenger for our love, you said 'Indeed!' and raised your eyebrows as if you were trying to keep some horrible thought hidden behind the wall of your brow. If you love me, Modibo, lower the wall and let me see your thought."

"You know I love you, Enaharo. You have been father and brother to me."

"And you have been son and brother to me. I know your heart and know it is full of love and honesty. I know how you weigh your words before you give them breath. That is why your hesitation to speak now frightens me."

Iago nodded. "Then let me be quick to say that I think Michael Cassio is honest."

"So do I. Go on."

"I would rather not, Enaharo. You ask me to utter my thoughts. What if my thoughts are vile and false? No man's breast is so pure that it is not tainted by unclean spots."

"Do you not trust me to be able to sort out gold from base metal?"

"Very well, but understand, too, that it is the plague of my nature to spy into abuses. Often I shape faults where none exist. More often than not, what I think is real is truly false. Where I see faults, you would see nothing at all. I do not let you know my thoughts because it would not serve your quiet and your goodness, nor my manhood, honesty, or wisdom."

"What does that mean?"

"A good name in man and woman, Enaharo, is the immediate jewel of their souls. Whoever steals my purse steals trash, but he that takes from me my good name robs me of that which will not enrich him and will make me poor indeed."

"Will you get to the point? I want to know what you are thinking, Modibo."

"I am thinking, Enaharo, that you should beware of jealousy. It is the green-eyed monster which mocks the meat it feeds on. I would rather defend London from the Saracens than defend my soul from jealousy!"

Othello shook his head. "Do you think I should be jealous because I see a man leaving from my wife? Do you think I need be jealous because other men think my wife beautiful, because she speaks, sings, plays and dances well and loves company? Did not every man in the realm have the opportunity to make her his wife before I came, including Michael Cassio? But she had eyes and she chose me. No, Modibo. I must see with my eyes before I doubt her, and even should I doubt her, I must have proof."

Iago smiled with relief. "I cannot tell you how glad your words make me. Now, I can speak more frankly, assured as I am that you will not believe my words merely because they are my words. You are quite right to ask for proof, and I have none. However, I would advise you to look to your wife. Observe her well with Cassio. Although you are older, I have more experience with women. I have observed these white women well and it is my opinion that they let heaven see what they would not show their husbands. A white woman will not leave something undone. She will merely keep it unknown."

"Is that true?"

Iago looked at him, incredulous. "Didn't she deceive her father to marry you?"

Othello nodded. "Her father pointed this out, also."

"She is so young, yet she skillfully sealed her father's eyes as close as oak. He suspected nothing and when it was revealed could only blame witchcraft." He stopped suddenly. "Forgive me, I have said enough, perhaps too much."

"I am indebted to you forever."

"You owe me nothing but your love."

"That you shall have always."

"Then, may I impose on your patience for one more thought?" Iago asked.

"It is no imposition. It is a favor you do me."

"I have never understood why the lady declined marriage with someone of her own complexion. I wonder if she, being of an excitable nature, was seeking an adventure of the spirit. Or perhaps she merely sought to anger her father. It is my fear that in a few months the appeal of the exotic and the different will have loosened its hold and she will awake one morning and be repulsed by that same blackness that she now finds so fascinating."

Othello shook his head in sadness. "I am ashamed something so obvious did not occur to me."

"Do not be hasty," Iago said quickly. "Time provides proof and disproof. Wait. I agree that Cassio should be returned to his rank. He has such ability for it. But nothing is lost if you wait a while to do so. In that way you can see how your lady reacts. But for now, do not put stock in my words. They are only words. Deeds are, however, another matter."

"Thank you, Modibo. I will do as you suggest."

"Good. Well, I must go."

Before Othello could bid him farewell, he was gone.

Chapter Fifteen

Iago Waters the Seeds

Though the sun shone brightly that day, a chill burned at the edges of Othello's heart, that heart he had always trusted as truth. Now he did not know what emotion to believe, or thought to cling to.

As he moved about the castle inspecting the battlements and his men, he kept seeing Michael Cassio fleeing from the garden at his approach. Would an innocent man have acted so? And what sort of man would use a woman to plead his cause?

But Othello's anger was stopped when he remembered that he had used another to plead his cause to Desdemona. Surely there were those who would have wondered why he had not been man enough to speak for himself? But there was a difference. **He was black and did not have the soft parts of conversation that those familiar with ladies' chambers had.** White women needed pretty words before their hearts would open. Perhaps it was all women. He did not know.

When noon came and the men went into the Great Hall for dinner, Othello declined to join them. Where once his stomach had always been ready to be filled with food and ale, there was now a dull aching which he feared nothing could assuage. Why had someone not warned him that love was a disruption of carefully wrought order, that love seared the soul more swiftly than a sword's slash drew blood. Why had someone not told him that giving up his loneliness for the comfort of union also meant becoming prey to the terror of chaos when union threatened to be split.

Love promised to make the heart soar as the falcon soared on winds only it felt. But all that soared had to eventually come to earth and plod through dust and mud, and withstand storms and winds through which no falcon could soar. But he was new to soaring. Could he endure a storm another man might not have noticed?

What would he do if Desdemona were saying to Michael Cassio words he thought she said only to him. But that was nonsense. Desdemona would never do such. Yet, as he had made his rounds through the castle that morning, he had not seen either Cassio or Desdemona. That could mean nothing — or everything.

As the sun passed the meridian and made its way deeper into the afternoon, Othello descended farther into exile from his love. Doubt became more trustworthy than knowledge, suspicion more a companion than affirmation. By the time he rode through the forest to the manor house, his head was pounding with the insistence of a waterfall.

"Is my lord not well?" Desdemona asked anxiously when she saw Othello stagger into the house.

"I have a headache," he whispered.

"Here. **Let me bind it tight with my handkerchief. That will make it all better within the hour.**" She took the handkerchief he had given her from her bosom and went to tie it around his head.

"**That handkerchief is too small,**" Othello said, annoyed, knocking her hand away and the handkerchief to the floor.

"I am sorry my lord is not feeling well," Desdemona responded. "Come. Let us go within and you can lie down. Emily will make you some camomile tea and I will stroke your brow. No pain would dare resist my touch." Desdemona took his arm and led him gently into the bedroom and closed the door.

Emily had been preparing supper at the fireplace. As she turned to put a pot of water for the tea above the flames, she saw the dusk-red handkerchief on the floor. Without thinking, she picked it up and put it in her pocket.

Chapter Sixteen

Ashaki

She thought of herself as Ashaki — Beautiful.

Emily. It was pretty enough, but not a name that made her feel she lived in her skin. She wondered if the white people thought it was her real name. Probably. Seldom had any of them expressed curiosity about where she came from. Did it occur to them that she, Enaharo, and Modibo missed their homes? None of the white people, not even Desdemona, knew that she and Iago and Othello had other names. They had never talked about it but she was sure they all agreed: To tell their true names to a white person would be to give their spirits away.

Ashaki moved easily and confidently along the path from the manor house to the castle. It was night, but she did not need a torch to cleave a path through the darkness for her. The body had ways of seeing that eyes did not. She did not fear the darkness as the white people did. She often wondered why they did not trust their god to protect them from spirits. Maybe their god was overworked because there was only him and his son. The world was far too vast for one god alone.

She wondered if that was why Enaharo looked ill. He had turned his back on his gods and made the crossing sign of their god. But that was not all. He had married a child, a child as beautiful and exuberant as spring — but a child. If he had talked with Ashaki as he used to, she would have told him.

But what? And how much? Would she have told him that a marriage needed more than love, that it needed also a oneness that came from memories shared by the living and the ancestors. Would she have told him he could only trust a woman who was not afraid of the night? But he had not asked and she was hurt.

Once inside the castle, she went to the room she shared with Modibo. He was not there, which was no surprise. She had learned not to ask where he had been — or with whom. It was better not to know than to be burdened with knowledge she could not use.

Thus she was surprised when, a few moments later, the door opened and he walked in. She sat on a bench before the fireplace, and after exchanging greetings, he came and sat beside her.

"So, how are the newlyweds?" he wanted to know.

She shook her head. "I am not sure. He did not come home for dinner at noon. Did he dine in the Great Hall?"

Modibo shook his head. "He'll never dine there again as long as Lord Bertrand breathes."

"Wouldn't you think that a man just married

would want to be with his bride as much as possible?"

"Perhaps something came up with the men."

"And if it had, wouldn't you have known?"

"True. Did he dine at home this evening?"

"I wouldn't say he dined. He came in complaining of a pain in his head." And it was then she remembered. Reaching in the pocket of her apron, she pulled out the handkerchief. "Oh, dear."

"What's the matter?" Iago said.

"It is the handkerchief Enaharo gave to Desdemona for a wedding present."

"Is that so?" he responded, his voice charged with interest. "And how did it get into your hands?"

"When he came in this evening complaining of the pain in his head, Desdemona offered to wrap his head in the handkerchief. He became annoyed and knocked it from her hand. Her attention was focused on him and she led him to the bedroom to lie down. I picked up the handkerchief, thinking I would return it to her later. I had forgotten I had it until this very moment."

Modibo took it from her. "I have to see Enaharo first thing in the morning. I'll return it then."

"I have to be there also — to prepare breakfast. Give it back. She is probably going out of her mind wondering where it is."

"I said I would return it. If Desdemona asks

if you have seen it, say nothing." His voice was as cold and flat as a winter sky.

"Where're you going?" she asked as he got up.

"I need to bait a trap," he responded.

She looked at him, shrugged, and he was out the door.

Quickly he made his way through the castle and down to the barracks where the men slept. Quietly he stepped among them until he found Michael Cassio. He waited a moment until he was certain Michael was soundly asleep. Then, taking the handkerchief, he placed it by Cassio's head. And as swiftly as he had come, he disappeared back into the shadows.

Chapter Seventeen

The Seeds Sprout

The next morning Iago was at the manor house before Emily. Othello always awoke with the sun and Iago found him walking in the garden.

"Good morning," Iago greeted him in their native tongue.

"What brings you here so early?" Othello asked without returning the greeting. "All is well at the castle?"

There was an unanticipated coolness in Othello's manner.

"I was concerned about you," Iago responded hesitantly.

"Well you should be. I have not had a moment's peace since we spoke yesterday morning."

"I am sorry to hear it."

"It is all your fault," Othello replied, his voice trembling with anger.

"Mine?"

"Yes, yours. If a man has been robbed and doesn't know that anything has been stolen, if no one tells him, then he has not been robbed at all. I knew nothing and I suspected even less that there might be anything between my wife and Cassio. Because of you I now see deep shadows though there is no sun to make them."

Iago was taken aback by the rage. "I did not mean to so upset you."

"Is that so? It is too late for that. I demand you give me proof that I can see or you will wish you had been born a dog than answer my awakened wrath! And if you have no proof, then you have slandered and tortured me. And if that be so, abandon all remorse."

Iago shook his head. "I fear I made a mistake. To be direct and honest is not safe. I have learned my lesson. From now on, I'll love no friend if love breeds such anger." He turned to go.

"No. Wait," Othello called, his voice calmer. "My anger is displaced from the message to the messenger. Forgive me."

Iago nodded. "I can understand how you feel."

"I doubt it. One moment I think my wife is honest. The next, I think she is not. One moment I think you are honest and the next I am convinced that you are not. Her name was as fresh as the face of the Virgin. Now it is as begrimed and black as my own face. I do not know any longer what is real and what is illusion, what is true and what is false."

"I am sorry I ever uttered a word, but having done so, perhaps I can give you evidence that will lead directly to the door of truth."

"I find that I want you to speak while fearing to listen. Go on, but be quick."

"I will be frank. I do not like this. I speak only because foolish honesty and naive love led me to speak yesterday. Just this past evening I went to the barracks to check on the men. I happened to notice Michael Cassio as he was tossing and turning in his sleep. Thinking he might have been taken ill, I knelt beside him. There are a kind of men so loose of soul, that in their sleeps they mutter their affairs. Cassio is one. Thus, I heard him say, 'Sweet Desdemona, let us be wary. Let us hide our loves.' And then, he reached out and grabbed my hand, squeezed it and cried, 'O sweet creature!' Then he pulled me toward him and kissed me hard and sought to lay his leg over my thigh and cried, 'Cursed fate that gave you to the black one!' "

"Oh, my God!" moaned Othello.

"Do not take it so to heart. It was only a dream."

"And do we not relive in our dreams what we live while awake?" Othello countered.

"Do not jump to conclusions yet. Answer me this: Doesn't your wife have a handkerchief as red as death on a battlefield?"

"It was my wedding gift to her."

"The pity. I think I saw such a handkerchief by Cassio's head last evening as he called out to her and cursed you in his sleep."

"If what you say is true, I'll kill her! All my love is now blown to heaven. It is gone. Arise, black vengeance, from your hollow cell. Yield up, love, your crown and throne to hate."

"Do not be hasty, Enaharo."

"My rage is like a torrential stream that will never ebb to humble love. Never!"

"What would you have me do?" Iago offered.

"I want you to come to me this day and tell me that Cassio is not alive."

"It is done, but, let her live."

"Damn her! My one prayer is that I will be furnished with some swift means of death for the white devil."

Chapter Eighteen

Othello Confronts Desdemona

"Have you seen my handkerchief?" Desdemona asked Emily as she came into the main room of the house. Emily was cooking at the fireplace.

"Handkerchief?" she responded nervously.

"Yes. The one red as sorrow my lord gave me. I can't find it anywhere."

"I haven't seen it."

"I would rather have lost a purse full of money," Desdemona said, worried.

Emily turned toward the fireplace so Desdemona would not see the uneasiness on her face.

"Have you seen my lord this morning?" Desdemona asked.

"He and my husband were talking in the garden when I arrived. I thought I heard Iago leave a few moments ago but Othello has not come in. Perhaps the two left together and I did not hear."

At that moment the door opened and Othello walked in. "Emily. Good morning. And good morning to you, also, Desdemona."

Emily heard a coolness in his voice and wondered what was wrong. Desdemona appeared to notice nothing. Or if she noticed, pretended not to. "Good morning, my lord," she said warmly. "How is the pain in your head this morning?"

"It has passed but I fear I may be catching a cold. Lend me your handkerchief."

Desdemona pulled a handkerchief from her pocket and offered it to him.

"This is not the one I gave you."

"I don't have it on me," she replied calmly.

"I see," he said cooly. "That is too bad. I hope nothing has happened to it. An Egyptian charmer gave that handkerchief to my mother. This Egyptian, I am told, was a woman of powers so great that she read people's thoughts before they opened their mouths. She told my mother that as long as she kept that handkerchief, my father would love her totally. But if she ever lost it, or gave it away, my father would grow to hate her and would look for another woman. When my mother lay dying, she gave the handkerchief to me and told me to give it to my wife, which I have done. If that handkerchief should ever be lost or should you give it away, the consequences will be far beyond any that you could imagine."

Desdemona paled. "I — I did not know."

"My mother told me there is magic in the weave of the handkerchief. An ancient sibyl wove it from silk spun by sacred worms. It gets its great power from having been dyed in mummified maidens' hearts. You would be wise to look after it well."

Desdemona gasped. "I wish to God I had never seen it."

"Oh? And why is that?"

"Why do you choose this moment to tell me? Why did you not tell me when you gave it to me?"

"Is it lost?" Othello asked sharply, his voice rising. "Is it gone? Speak! Where is it?"

"It is not lost."

"Then, get it. Let me see it."

"I could, but I won't right at this moment," she said, breezily. "You are trying to distract me from what is on my mind. Will you restore Michael today?"

"Bring me the handkerchief."

"You know yourself that he does not deserve to be banished so from your presence and your trust," she went on quickly, trying to distract him.

"The handkerchief!"

"Talk to me of Michael."

"The handkerchief!"

"You seem to forget that Cassio entrusted his future in his love for you, has shared dangers with you — "

"The handkerchief!"

Desdemona opened her mouth to say — she knew not what — anything that would distract him from his fixation on the handkerchief. Whatever words would have come forth were stopped in her throat by the murderous rage she saw in his face. She stepped back, frightened. "My lord?" she whispered, her voice scarcely audible.

Perhaps it was the softness in her voice, but, as awakening from a dream, he saw the fear in her face. What was he doing that the one he loved more than life should now be afraid of him? His mouth moved but no words would come. He wanted to tell her he was sorry. But why was she pleading on behalf of Michael Cassio like a priest for a sinning soul? And though he knew she couldn't, he wanted her to produce the handkerchief. Worse, she knew she could not. If she had apologized and said she knew not where it was, he might have been assuaged. But she lied. Why would she lie except to hide a truth more foul? Like a fire flickering to its end, but finding an unconsumed knot of fuel, flares into life again, so rage returned to his eyes. He screamed, pounded his fist into the palm of his hand, spun around, and was out the door, slamming it behind him.

Desdemona burst into tears. Emily hurried across the room and held her tightly. "A man is nothing but a stomach and a woman but food. They eat us greedily, and when they are full, they belch us."

Desdemona shook her head. "I will not believe such of Othello. Did you not say that he and Iago were conferring in the garden even before you came this morning?"

"This is true."

"Perhaps Iago brought him a message from the King. Some affair of state or war has puddled his clear spirit. Is it not sometimes true that a man will quarrel with the inconsequential when he is worried about something greater? More than once I have pricked my finger and such a small pain has made me forget the well-being of all the other members of my body."

"I hope you are right. But I have never seen Othello act so. I did not know he was capable of such jealousy."

"Nor I. Have I inadvertently given him cause to be suspicious of my devotion, Emily?"

"Jealousy needs no cause, and it is impervious to reason or sense. It is a monster begot upon itself, born on itself."

"I pray God will keep that monster from Othello's soul. I must find that handkerchief, Emily. Will you help me search the house for it? Please?"

It was all Emily could do to keep silent. And keeping silent, she wondered why she did not speak. It would have been so simple to say, "My husband has the handkerchief." But she was sure he would return the handkerchief soon and that would clear up everything. She suspected that he wanted to show it to a seamstress and surprise Emily with one of her own. Why else would he have been so eager to keep it?

If he had not returned it by that evening she would be forced to say something. But what would Enaharo and Desdemona think of her for not having spoken sooner? How could they ever trust her again if they knew that one word from her would have stopped their pain? No, she would wait. Modibo would return the handkerchief. If not this evening, then surely tomorrow.

She thought she knew why he had wanted it.

He wanted to surprise her with a copy of the handkerchief. It had unusual stitching. He had taken it to a seamstress.

Emily smiled weakly. That had to be the reason. It had to be.

Chapter Nineteen

Elsewhere

When Michael Cassio awoke that morning, he instinctively reached for the handkerchief by his head, thinking it his own. Not yet wholly awake, he thrust it in his pocket and went out into the yard.

He did not know what to do with himself. Having been demoted to an ordinary soldier, he was ashamed to be around the men. He wandered down to the garden, hoping to chance upon Desdemona and ask if she had had any success in persuading Othello to reinstate him.

She was not there and he doubted she would come. He sat anyway. Here, at least, his shame would not be exposed to anyone who chose to cast a glance his way.

He had not been sitting long when he saw a woman coming. For a moment his heart lifted, thinking it was Desdemona. But as she came closer he recognized Belinda, whom, he remembered guiltily, he had not seen since that night.

"Hello, stranger," she greeted him.

He managed a smile in response. "How goes it with you?"

"Feeling neglected."

"And why is that?"

"You have been ignoring me."

"My apologies, Belinda. In fact, I was planning to come see you today."

"Is that so?"

"Indeed, I was. I have been pressed with leaden thoughts."

She sat down beside him. "Perhaps you should let me extract the dross from your mind." She leaned into him to kiss him on the cheek, but feeling a bulge in the pocket of his jacket, she reached inside and pulled out the handkerchief.

"And where did this come from?" she demanded to know.

Michael looked at it. "Why, I don't know," he responded with genuine surprise. "I don't know. I remember grasping a handkerchief when I awoke this morning. I assumed it was one of my own and put it in my pocket without looking at it."

"And how came it to be on your pallet?"

He shrugged. "I don't know."

"Well, I do," she said emphatically. "Do you think I did not look out from the kitchen yesterday and see you sitting here in the garden with the General's wife? Do you think I did not see you slink away at the General's approach? I thought it strange that you had time to meet the Lady Desdemona but did not have time for me."

"You don't understand," he interrupted. "Desdemona is helping me regain my lieutenancy. That is all."

Belinda put the handkerchief in her bosom. "Is that so?"

"Yes, it is. I swear it."

Belinda got up. "Well, I think Desdemona or some other woman gave it to you. I think I will flaunt it about and see whose face flames."

"Don't do this to me," Michael pleaded. "I have enough problems."

Belinda smiled. "Will I see you tonight, Michael Cassio?" she teased.

He nodded weakly.

❖ ❖ ❖

About that same time in a corner of the barracks, Iago was speaking to Richard. "A word with you?"

Richard nodded. "What's on your mind?"

"More drastic action is needed if we are to remain free of Cassio as our lieutenant."

"Oh?"

"I fear the General is planning to reinstate him."

"And that does not suit you," Richard remarked flatly.

"Not at all."

"How much does it not suit you?"

"You will be astonished at how deeply I want the matter resolved."

"And how much resolution are you seeking?" Richard wanted to know, though the answer was obvious.

"I fear the situation requires a permanent one. Time is short. It is a simple matter if one soldier kills another. It is entirely another if a soldier slays one of his officers. I do not know it for a fact but I thought I understood the General to say that he was going to reinstate Cassio tomorrow."

"Then it is safer if Michael Cassio has no tomorrow."

Chapter Twenty

Othello Finds the Handkerchief

The day passed at the pace of a funeral cortege. Othello moved through it as numb as a mourner whose grief is as endless as the sky. However, it was not clear to him for what or whom he grieved. Was it the loss of the only love of his life? Or was it the grief that is rage afraid to hear its voice? How could he have been so naive as to believe that one as young and beautiful as she would truly love someone so much older, someone who while not ugly was far from handsome? And how could he have so deceived himself to believe that a woman as white as the new moon would love one as black as the heavens surrounding it? Had he thought she would not notice, or noticing, not be repulsed?

He had been in Europe too long. He had come to believe he was one of them. He spoke Italian as well as any Italian, Spanish as if he had heard the language while yet entombed in his mother's belly, and English as well as the Prince's tutor. In whatever country, in whoever's service, he had become as one of them. Or so he thought.

He remembered now the times Modibo and

Ashaki had begged for the three of them to return to Songhay, or even Cairo. He had refused. In his mind he had derided them for their unwillingness or inability to adapt to whatever fortune sent their way. Modibo and Ashaki still believed in the old gods, and, in private, preferred to express themselves in the language of their youth. But Modibo had known what he was learning only now: Appearance is reality.

It did not matter how many of their languages he spoke. It did not matter how many of their customs he observed. They judged his reality by his appearance. His deeds counted for little. Her own father, a man whom he had sat next to at meals every day for months, had never seen beyond his unavoidable blackness.

Yet, it had appeared that Lord Bertrand had been fond of him and had no untoward opinion about the blackness of his face, his thick lips and nose, the tight curls of his hair. But Lord Bertrand had loathed him for the very color of skin and racial peculiarities he appeared not to notice.

What kind of cruel game was that? Why would someone put such effort into making one believe what was not so? He did not understand, and because he didn't, he was afraid to believe anyone. Especially the daughter of a man who could lie so well, the same daughter who deceived her father as effortlessly as the father deceived a black man foolish enough to have trusted them both. He needed proof, something he could touch with his fingers, hold in his hands, something whose reality would not change when he blinked his eyes.

The proof came without being sought.

He had spent the morning going through the castle, pretending to check weapons and coats of mail, though there was no battle pending. People thought the life of a soldier was an exciting one. Little did they know that for a few weeks' excitement and danger, a soldier spent months, sometimes years, of torturous boredom, polishing what already shone, sharpening what was already lethal enough to slice the wind. Yet it was important that the men stay alert, especially when they were on watch. Othello had won more than one battle because he had known how to gauge when the enemy's boredom became carelessness.

He was walking through the inner yard of the castle where the servants were bringing provisions from the storeroom to the kitchen. There, tucked into the blouse of a very attractive young woman, he saw the red handkerchief glaring like sunlight off the helmet of a dead knight.

"You!" Othello roared so loudly that everyone stopped. He pointed at Belinda and yelled again. "Come here!"

Belinda looked around, hoping all that rage was directed at someone else.

"Yes! You!"

She hurried to him and curtsied. "General?"

"Where did you get this?" he demanded to know, snatching the handkerchief from her blouse.

Belinda kept her eyes lowered. So it's true, she thought. Desdemona *had* given the handkerchief to Michael.

"Get what, sir?" she mumbled as she desperately tried to think of what to say.

"Are you stupid, girl? This handkerchief!"

"Oh, that," she said, giggling nervously. "I — I — I found it."

Othello grabbed her chin and pushed it up so she was forced to look into his enraged face. "Lie to me and . . ." He seized her neck and squeezed. "I will break your neck more easily than you can break a dry branch to throw into the fireplace. Now. Where did you get this handkerchief?"

Tears came to her eyes. Why should she lie to cover up for Michael Cassio? If he was seeing the General's wife behind her back, he deserved whatever came to him. "It was a gift, sir."

"Who gave it to you?"

"Michael Cassio, sir."

Othello moaned as if a skilled assassin had slipped a blade between his ribs. He released Belinda and the handkerchief slipped from his fingers and floated to the ground. Othello put his hand to his head as pain seized it.

He staggered through the courtyard and outside to where his horse was tethered. Perhaps that was why he had become a soldier and become so good at it. In war life and death were clearly marked and clearly seen. And each was as real as it appeared to be. He understood death. He did not understand love — and would no longer try.

Chapter Twenty-one

Othello and Desdemona

The slow-dying rays of the early summer sun still lighted the house when Othello entered. Emily sat alone on a bench near the fireplace where the food was being kept warm on the banked coals.

"Enaharo," she greeted him.

"Where is Desdemona?" he demanded.

Emily pointed with her head toward the back. "In the garden."

Othello visibly relaxed. "She has been here all day?"

Emily nodded.

"Have there been any visitors?"

"None. What do you mean by these questions? Your suspicions choke the air."

"Michael Cassio has not been here today?"

"He has not."

"Yesterday when I saw the two of them sitting together in the garden on the castle ground, what did they speak of?"

"Nothing except his remorse at having disgraced himself and lost your respect."

"Did they ever whisper?"

"Never."

"Did they ever ask you to move out of hearing's range?"

"Never."

"Not even on the pretense of getting her gloves, a fan? Nothing?"

"Never."

"And would you tell me the truth, Ashaki?"

Tears came to her eyes. "I do not know you. I knew once a man who looked like you, remarkably so. Enaharo was his name, and such a man he was. If he had been younger or I had been older — who knows? This man could look on the face of any man and any woman and see a goodness others overlooked. Even his enemies wanted to call him friend. But you I do not know. You look on goodness and see evil. You gaze at innocence and call it sin. You behold purity and declaim perdition."

Othello looked at her with disdain. "I ask a question and receive a sermon. The fact you did not answer simply is answer enough."

He turned and walked out of the house and back to the garden.

"My lord!" Desdemona said excitedly on seeing him. "I am so glad you have come home for supper. I have missed you." She moved toward him, arms open, but slowed her step, then lowered her arms as she saw the anger in his face. "What is it, my lord?"

"What is it, my lord?" he mocked her.

"Why do you hurt me so? I understand a fury in your words, but not the words."

"What are you?" he asked coldly.

"Your wife, my lord. Your true and loyal wife."

"Swear you are honest," he roared suddenly.

"Heaven knows it."

"Heaven knows you are false as hell."

"To whom, my lord? With whom? How am I false?"

"Desdemona!" he cried out. "How could you? If it had pleased God to try me with afflictions, if God had rained all kinds of sores and shames on my head, steeped me in poverty to the very lips, made captive my body and all my hopes, I would have been able to find a drop of patience somewhere in my soul. But in your soul I have stored my heart and given you the power by which I live or die and it is there the rodents come in and tear holes in the sacks, leaving the grain to trickle out and rot." He looked at her, his eyes glazed with tears. "You are so beautiful. My senses ache at the very sight of you. How I wish you had never been born."

Desdemona looked up at him, her eyes pleading. "What sin have I committed against you?"

"What sin?" he asked, incredulous, his rage returning. "What sin? you ask. How could you not know? Heaven must close its nose and the moon shuts it eyes. The promiscuous wind that kisses all it meets is still. And you dare ask what sin you have committed?"

She shook her head sadly. "Heaven knows you do me wrong."

"You have been faithful to me?"

"As faithful as the sun to its track around the earth."

"You lie so smoothly. Leave me. I cannot bear to look on your face any longer. Leave me."

Desdemona looked at him but he would not return her gaze. Tears filled her eyes as she tried to understand. Was it not part of the nature of things that dark clouds, lightning, and thunder gave warning of an impending storm? But she had seen no clouds, nor winced at a flash of lightning, or shuddered at the roll of thunder. Yet the sun was hidden from view and the wind was chilly while the sky was denuded of clouds. She wanted to speak but did not know the words that could turn anger to melody. Even if she had known and had spoken them, she feared he would have closed his ears like the castle gates being shut against an onrushing enemy.

She walked slowly from the garden and into the house, her head bowed.

"What's the matter with my lord?" Emily asked her.

"With who?"

"With my lord, madam."

"Who is your lord?" Desdemona asked blankly.

"He that is yours."

"I have none. My mother once had a maid called Barbara. She was in love, but the one she loved became mad and left her. Barbara sang a song and it was on her lips as she died. I cannot get that song out of my mind tonight.

"The poor soul sat sighing by a sycamore tree,
    Sing all a green willow;

Her hand on her bosom, her head on her knee,
  Sing willow, willow, willow:
The fresh streams ran by her, and murmured her
  moans;
  Sing willow, willow, willow;
Her salt tears fell from her, and softened the stones;
  Sing willow, willow, willow;

Sing all a green willow must be my garland,
  Let nobody blame him; his scorn I approve, —

"No, that's not how it goes." She stopped and listened. "What is that knocking I hear?" she asked, her voice hollow and distant.

"It is the wind," Emily said, though she had heard nothing.

Desdemona resumed singing.

"I called my love false love; but what said he then?
  Sing willow, willow, willow:
If I court more women, you'll couch with more men.

"My eyes itch, Emily, Does that mean I am going to cry?"

Emily was not sure she herself was not going to cry. "It is neither here nor there."

"You know more about men than I. Tell me, please, are there women who are untrue to their husbands?"

Emily nodded. "There are some. No question."

"Would you do such for all the world?"

"Wouldn't you?"

Desdemona shook her head emphatically. "No, by this heavenly light."

Emily chuckled. "Nor I neither by this heavenly light. But I might do it in the dark."

Desdemona did not see the humor. "Would you be untrue for all the world?" she asked again, spreading her arms wide as if to summon the entire world.

"The world's a huge thing; it is a great price for a small vice."

Desdemona smiled then. "I don't think you would."

Emily demurred. "I am not sure. I would not do such a thing for gowns or petticoats or jewelry, but for the whole world. I daresay I would risk your purgatory for that."

"Damn me to hell if I would do such a wrong for the whole world."

"If you really want to know what I think, well, I think it is their husbands' faults if wives are untrue. It is they who curdle the milk with their suspicions and jealousies. It is they who want to keep us locked away from an admiring eye or a covetous and innocent smile. It is they who strike us when we will not take the bridles with which they seek to rein us. They do not think we are capable of anger and resentment. They do not think we would seek revenge on them as they would seek revenge on one who injured them in spirit or body. Husbands should know their wives have sense like them; we see and smell and our palates can taste both sweet and sour, just as husbands'. What is it that they do when they put others in our places? Do they do it for sport, for the fun of it? I believe so. Perhaps our affection for them breeds betrayal for they mistake our gift as their just due and no longer hold it of value. Or perhaps they wish to be affectionate with whomever pleases their eyes. Or perhaps men are frail and though they mean well, it is in their nature to err and expect our forgiveness. Are they so unmindful that they do not know that we, too, desire sport? Do they not know that we, too, are frail? Husbands should learn to use us well. Else let them know, the ills we do, their ills instruct us so."

Emily hoped her words would have sparked some light in Desdemona's dull eyes. But she saw none. It was as if the child had not heard.

"Good night, Emily. I'll see you in the morrow — either here or in heaven."

"What do you mean?" Emily asked, frightened.

"Good night, Emily. You must go now." Desdemona kissed her gently on each cheek and with slow steps, went into the bedroom, closing the door behind her.

Emily stared at the closed door for a moment, then left the house and went slowly toward the castle.

Chapter Twenty-two

Murder

The Great Hall was almost empty. Michael Cassio sat alone at a table in the rear. Throughout the day he had waited expectantly for some word from Desdemona. There had been none. He was not entirely surprised. Several times that day he had seen Othello moving through the castle, a rage in his stride. Not even in battle did he display such emotion. Such anger did not bode well for Michael's future.

He looked up to see Iago and his friend, Richard, approaching. Michael's spirits lifted. Iago was as close to Othello, if not closer than Desdemona. Perhaps he had some news.

"Gentlemen!" Michael greeted them.

"May we join you?" Iago inquired.

"Please. By all means. You bring word, perhaps?" Michael was annoyed with himself for being overeager.

"Word?" Iago echoed.

Michael's face fell. "Then, there is none."

"Word?" Richard repeated sarcastically.

"Do you mock me, sir?" Michael asked, irritated. "This matter is no concern of yours."

"It is of more concern to me than anybody," came the reply. "Are you so naive as to think the men don't know that you've asked the General's wife to do on your behalf what you are too gutless to do yourself? Do you think we want a man like that as our lieutenant? But I have a more personal reason for wanting to see you shivering in the cold. You tried to kill me once. If you are made lieutenant again, what is to say that you won't succeed the next time."

Michael leaped to his feet. "Then let us settle the matter now," he said, pulling his knife, his frustration and anguish glad to have a target.

"Nothing would suit me better," Richard responded, pulling his own knife.

"Gentlemen! Gentlemen!" Iago shouted, stepping between the two.

Michael pushed Iago aside. "I know you mean well, but I see how the men look at me now. If I am going to regain my status and their respect, I must prove myself to be a man and this one seems to have offered himself for the honor."

Richard grinned and, in so doing, was not alert to the speed with which Michael Cassio could move. Michael feinted with his knife to the left, and as Richard moved to defend himself, Michael thrust to the right, driving the knife into Richard's side.

"I am killed!" Richard shouted, grasping his side and seeking to staunch the flow of blood with his hands. "I am killed!" he repeated, slumping to the floor.

Men hurried into the Great Hall from outside. They surrounded Michael and the fallen Richard. Iago insinuated himself into the crowd, his knife held tightly in his hand, his hand at his side. No one saw him stab Michael with an upward thrust.

"I am stabbed," Michael screamed, grabbing his back. "I am stabbed." He staggered and slid slowly to the floor beside Richard.

"Who has done this?" Iago shouted, as if seeking justice on Michael's would-be murderer.

Just then Richard opened his syes. He looked up at Iago. "You who appear to be friend to every man are the enemy of all," he said haltingly.

"If not for you, Michael Cassio would not now lie wounded!" Iago shouted and plunged his knife into Richard's chest. "Murderer!" he shouted. He leaped to his feet and stared into the faces of the horror-stricken men. "Who here among you was working with Richard and just now tried to finish on Cassio what Richard failed at?"

Just then Michael moaned. "Iago," he said, "you seek justice while I lie wounded. I beg you, let justice languish a while."

"Forgive me," Iago said, bending over Michael. "Quick! Someone get the doctor. The wound seems to be only a superficial cut."

"It burns like death."

"Then it is not death," Iago answered. "Death does not feel, Michael Cassio. Death does not feel. You will live."

"Thanks to you."

"I deserve no thanks," Iago responded. "None at all."

Chapter Twenty-three

The Last Kiss

Othello did not know how long he sat in the garden after Desdemona left. It could have been an hour or an eon. Grief had substituted itself for time. While the stars and the moon moved across the night sky, grief held him suspended outside time where there was no forward or backward.

In grief he was more alone than he had ever thought possible. No one had warned him that to love meant to risk an aloneness so deep and so vast that death would appear convivial. He thought he understood now why, in his country, a man had many wives. There was no danger he would give his soul away to one. Among his people marriage was not so personal. There was affection between a man and his wives, but there was not this concentration of spirit when two focused only on each other.

It was a dangerous way for two people to be. All meaning and significance was lodged in the other. What if that other should decide the meaning of yesterday was of no consequence today? That was where his people were very wise. "Guard your spirit," they said. He remembered the old ones reciting legends about women who stole men's spirits. Without his spirit, a man died.

That was what love was. A thief that plundered a man's soul and pillaged his spirit, leaving him as empty and charred as the remains of a town after the rampage of an indifferent enemy. Well, if she would not return his spirit to him, he would have to make certain she could no longer hold it within herself. If he could not have it, neither could she.

When he entered the bedroom, she was asleep. In the light of the lantern by the bed he gazed down at her, the smooth whiteness of her skin, the silken softness of her dark hair. He did not want to disturb her beauty with blood. He bent and kissed her lightly on the cheek. He knew then that killing her would not end his love but return it. In death his spirit would be restored and once restored he would love her. Then he would be whole again.

"Othello?" Desdemona whispered, opening her eyes.

"It is I, my love," he whispered.

"Are you coming to bed?"

"Have you said your prayers tonight, Desdemona?"

She looked at him curiously. "Yes, my lord."

"If there is any sin for which you have not asked forgiveness, do it now."

Her eyes opened wide. "What do you mean by that?"

"I do not want to kill your unprepared soul."

"Kill? Why are you talking of killing?"

"Because it is the deed to consecrate my love."

She sat up in the bed, her eyes filling with tears. "Then heaven have mercy on me!"

"Amen!" he responded.

"Please do not kill me."

"Think about your sins."

"They are loves I bear to you," she pleaded.

"And for that you will die."

"That death's unnatural that kills for loving."

"Peace and be still!"

"I beg of you, my lord, won't you at least tell me what this is about?"

"Don't you know?" he exclaimed. "How can you not know?"

"Perhaps I know and do not know that I know. Please, my lord. I beg of you!"

"That handkerchief which I so loved and gave to you, you gave to Cassio."

"By my life and soul, I did not!" she exclaimed emphatically. "Send for Cassio. Ask him."

"Be careful, my love. Be careful that you do not lie on your deathbed."

"I do not lie. I have never offended you, nor have I ever loved Cassio except as the brother I never had. And I never gave him any sign of affection."

"Do not lie to me, woman. I saw that handkerchief in the bosom of another woman who told me with her lips that it was a gift to her from Michael Cassio."

"He found it then. I never gave it to him. Send for

him. Let him tell you how he came by the handkerchief."

"That is not possible. His mouth is stopped if Iago was as good as his word."

She gasped. "Is he dead?"

"If not at this moment, the next."

She broke into tears. "No, no, no. How did matters reach such a place as this?"

"You dare weep for him in front of me?"

"No, my lord. I weep for you."

"For me!" he roared, indignant. "I, the one sinned against, am to be pitied by the sinner?" His large hands grabbed her throat. "Save your tears for yourself." He squeezed with all his great strength. She struggled for a moment, her eyes growing larger and larger. She looked at him, hoping he would look at her, and seeing, remember himself and her. But his eyes were glazed, drunken with passion for something that was neither of them. Still, as darkness slowly covered her from within, Desdemona strained to speak, to tell him one last time, that now, even now, she loved him. But life flailed with her, seeking some outcropping to cling to. Finding none, it lost its grip and fell into the void from which all life came and to which all life returns.

Her body had been limp for a while before Othello's grip relaxed. He looked down at her, then pulled the lifeless body next to him with a tenderness as strong in its gentleness as the power of before. He rocked her back and forth, tears coursing down his face. He stroked her hair over and over and kissed her gently on the lips. "How I do love you," he whispered. "How I do love you."

"My lord?" came a voice from outside the door. "My lord!"

"What noise is this?" he called out, looking at Desdemona as if he thought it was she who had spoken.

"My lord?" came the voice again.

"Who's there?"

"It is I. Emily. I must speak with you."

"One moment."

He lay Desdemona down gently, covered her, and arranged her hair about her shoulders so it appeared she was asleep. Then he opened the door.

"How's Desdemona?" she asked, anxiously peering into the room.

"Why are you concerned?"

"She was talking strangely and sent me away." Emily tried to peer around him into the room. "She is well?"

"Indeed she is."

"I am glad to hear it because it has been an awful night."

"What do you mean?"

"There has been murder at the castle."

"Murder?" Othello asked excitedly. "What has happened?"

"I do not know the all of it but Richard and

Michael Cassio were involved in a fight and Richard was killed."

"Richard killed and Cassio killed?"

"No, Cassio was only wounded, and not seriously. He, Iago, and some of the other men are on their way here this very moment. I came ahead because I thought my lady would rather hear the news about Michael from me." Emily moved past Othello into the room. "It is odd she yet sleeps, she whose sleep is as light as a butterfly's kiss on the heart of a flower." Emily sat down on the edge of the bed. "Desdemona."

There was no answer.

Emily touched her arm and shook her. There was no response. "Oh, dear God!" she exclaimed. "What — what happened? Desdemona! Desdemona! Oh, dear God!"

Othello turned. "She is dead. I murdered her."

"I knew it! I knew it!" Emily screamed. "I knew I should not have left. She knew she was going to die and she tried to tell me so. What have you done, Enaharo? Have you gone mad?"

"She was false as water."

"You are as rash as fire. She was heavenly true."

"She was in love with Cassio. Ask your husband. He knew it well."

"Modibo?"

"Modibo!"

"He said she was untrue to you?"

"Yes, and with Cassio."

"My husband said that?"

"It was he that opened my eyes to what was going on around me."

"My husband."

"Why do you repeat yourself? Yes, your husband."

"He lied, I tell you. He lied."

Before she could continue, Iago, Michael, Lord Bertrand, and the Duke of Widdington entered the house, accompanied by a number of soldiers. Before anyone could speak, Emily went to her husband. "Othello said you told him Desdemona was untrue. Tell me you are not such a villain. Speak, for my heart is full."

Iago tried to smile. "I merely told him what I thought. What he found to be true and apt was up to him."

"But did you tell him she was untrue?"

"I did."

"You lied. You lied a wicked lie. Did you tell him she was unfaithful with Cassio?"

"Hold your tongue, woman."

"I will not. I cannot. Desdemona lies murdered in her bed."

"Murdered!" the men exclaimed. Lord Bertrand, Michael, and the Duke of Widdington rushed into the bedroom, pushing Othello aside.

Emily wailed loudly. "Your words created this murder, my husband."

"Nonsense!" Othello interrupted. "She was foul. I killed her because to allow her to live would have permitted sin to gain the victory. She had to die! Iago knows the truth, knows that she sealed her love for Cassio with the handkerchief I gave to her as the seal upon our love."

"Oh, oh, oh!" moaned Emily.

"Quiet!" Iago ordered her.

"It is all clear now and I will not be quiet. Let heaven and men and devils, let them all, all, all cry shame against me, but I must speak."

"I told you to be quiet!"

"And I said I will not! Enaharo! Enaharo! It is my fault. That handkerchief you took as proof of her unfaithfulness. Do you remember that she offered to bind your head with it to rid you of a headache?"

Othello thought and memory returned. "I do."

"And you knocked it from her hand, telling her it was too small?"

"That is so," he said softly, horror unfolding across his face. "Oh, dear God!" he moaned.

"She took you into the chamber that became her deathbed. I picked the handkerchief from the floor and put it in my pocket, thinking I would give it to her later. I forgot and my husband found it there when I returned to the castle. He took it from me. I thought he did so in order to make a copy for me."

"Shut up, woman!" Before anyone could move, Iago pulled his knife and plunged it into her chest.

Emily slumped to the floor and Iago fled through the door and outside.

"Get him!" Othello ordered, and the soldiers hastened into action.

Othello dropped to his knees beside Ashaki.

"Enaharo," she whispered. "She was as faithful to you as grass to the earth." And she died.

Othello held her tightly. "Ashaki," he said only loudly enough for her to hear, if she could have heard. "Please tell her that I loved her. I know when I get to the other side, one look of hers will hurl my soul from heaven and fiends will snatch it. And I will not mind. Whip me, devils! Blow me about in winds! Roast me in sulphur! Wash me in steep-down gulfs of liquid fire! Yet, even then, even then, I will love her."

Othello sat silently by the body. He might have sat there always had not the soldiers returned, Iago held tightly between them. The Duke of Widdington came out of the bedroom and went to Iago. Without warning he slapped him across the face, hard, once, twice.

"Speak," he ordered Iago.

A sneer coursed slowly across Iago's face. With a disdain all the more chilling because he spoke without emotion, he told the Duke of Widdington all that had taken place.

When he finished, the Duke went to Othello. "Iago has told me everything." He shook his head. "I do not know what to say to you. I do not know what to say about you."

"Call me an honorable murderer, for I did nothing in hate and all in honor. Speak of me as one that loved not wisely but too well."

"Is it true as Iago says that the two of you plotted to kill Michael Cassio?"

"We did."

"But what cause did I give you?" Michael broke in plaintively.

"None, Cassio, and I ask your pardon. But if you would be so kind as to satisfy my curiosity, how did you come by the handkerchief I gave to my wife?"

"I awoke and found it next to my head. Half asleep, I put it in my pocket and Belinda found it, thought it a gift to me from another woman, and took it."

The Duke said, "Iago has confessed that he planted the handkerchief by Cassio's sleeping head."

Othello shook his head slowly. "Has there ever been a fool such as I?" He looked at Iago. "Why, Modibo?" he asked in their native tongue. "Why?"

"It is not I, Enaharo. What I spoke you did not have to believe. It is not me or my words that are the villain here. Look to your own soul for the weakness."

Othello stared at him for a moment. He looked as if he were going to say something else, but without a word, he pulled his knife. As his arm descended, Iago moved and the blade went into Iago's shoulder. Othello pulled it out to deliver a more lethal wound, but two men grabbed his arm and wrested the knife from his hand.

Othello turned and walked slowly into the bedroom. He sat down on the side of the bed and looked at Desdemona. "I kissed you before I killed you. Now, I die upon a kiss," he whispered.

He kissed her unmoving lips with all the fury of the storm-swelled sea. Then reaching beneath the bed, took the sword he kept there and fell on it. Slowly he slumped dead across the body of the one he loved.

The men had seen it all through the open doorway and they were silent, not knowing what to say or think. The only sound was the soft weeping of Michael Cassio.

Finally, the Duke of Widdington spoke. "Go to the castle and tell the carpenters to build a gallows. I would have Iago hanged and dead by sunset." He put his arm around the shoulders of Lord Bertrand. "We must arrange the burial of your daughter."

With tears in his eyes Lord Bertrand looked at the Duke. "Woe is me, old friend, that I will treat her in death as I should have in life. Bury her and Othello in one grave, next to my wife. Lay Emily in a grave beside them. And leave a place for me. I do not think it will be long before I join them."

The Duke nodded. He motioned for men to go into the bedroom where they raised the bodies of Othello and Desdemona to their shoulders. In the outer room Emily's was raised on other shoulders.

Othello, Desdemona, and Emily were carried in solemn procession back to the castle.

Morning dawned, death-red, at the lip of the horizon.

Somewhere a cock crowed.

Another day began.

About the Author

Julius Lester is the award-winning author of books for both children and adults. About this novel Lester says, "In more than thirty years of writing, *Othello* was the most exciting project to work on. I couldn't wait to get up in the morning to write this book."

Lester's impressive backlist includes *To Be a Slave*, a Newbery Honor Book, *Tales of Uncle Remus*, an ALA Notable Book, *More Tales of Uncle Remus*, a *School Library Journal* Best Book, and *How Many Spots Does a Leopard Have?*

Mr. Lester lives in western Massachusetts, where he is a professor in the Department of Judaic and Near Eastern Studies at the University of Massachusetts.

Also by Julius Lester

To Be a Slave

❖

Black Folktales

❖

How Many Spots Does a Leopard Have?

❖

John Henry

❖

The Knee-High Man & Other Tales

❖

Long Journey Home: Stories from Black History

❖

*The Man Who Knew Too Much: A Moral
Tale from the Baila of Zambia*

❖

Tales of Uncle Remus

❖

The Last Tales of Uncle Remus

❖

More Tales of Uncle Remus

❖

Further Tales of Uncle Remus

Othello was typeset in Times Roman and Gill Sans
by N.K. Graphics, Inc., Keene, New Hampshire.
The display type was typeset in Kingsbury Condensed.
The book was printed on 55-lb. Renew Antique paper and
printed and bound by Berryville Graphics, Berryville, Virginia.
Production supervision by Heather Service.